The Web of Words

Exploring literature through language

*Ronald Carter and
Michael N. Long*

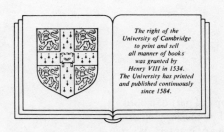

The right of the
University of Cambridge
to print and sell
all manner of books
was granted by
Henry VIII in 1534.
The University has printed
and published continuously
since 1584.

Cambridge University Press
Cambridge
New York   New Rochelle
Melbourne   Sydney

Published by the Press Syndicate of the University of Cambridge
The Pitt Building, Trumpington Street, Cambridge CB2 1RP
32 East 57th Street, New York, NY 10022, USA
10 Stamford Road, Oakleigh, Melbourne 3166, Australia

© Cambridge University Press 1987

First published 1987

Book designed by Peter Ducker MSTD

Printed in Great Britain
at the Bath Press, Avon

ISBN 0 521 27772 8   Student's Book
ISBN 0 521 33926 X   Teacher's Book
ISBN 0 521 30778 3   Cassette

WV

Contents

Thanks

This book has been extensively piloted in over a dozen countries: the most detailed piloting was undertaken in UK; Italy; Greece; West Germany; Singapore; Thailand; Hong Kong and Macau; Kenya; The Netherlands; The Philippines; Indonesia.

Many teachers have provided valuable comments, especially as a result of trialling the materials on British Council courses and in-service training programmes. It is impossible to acknowledge all contributors individually but special thanks go to Matthew Macmillan; Costas Evangelides; Luke Prodromou; Roy Boardman; Michael Toolan; David Birch; Christopher Brumfit; Mary Todd-Trimble; Peter Hill.

Special thanks are also due to John McRae and Roger Gower, both of whom provided pages of commentary. Both gave generously of their time and provided detailed criticisms to which we tried to respond and which helped us clarify many hazy areas. Of course, we do not wish to associate any of the above named with the final version. We alone are responsible for that. But we wish to thank them all sincerely for their time, interest and commitment. From Cambridge University Press thanks are also due to Peter Donovan and Margherita Baker who have given much insightful criticism and have demonstrated the necessary but often underestimated co-creative role of editors.

Introduction

There's a cool web of language winds us in

Robert Graves: 'The Cool Web'

For the teacher

Aims

In recent years the teaching of English language and the teaching of English literature have tended to coexist in many different ways especially where the language is being studied by non-native speakers of English. In some courses, literature has been omitted altogether because it was judged to be not absolutely practical and necessary to certain specific purposes in learning the language. In other courses, literature teaching has been dominant and at an advanced level students have studied more English literature than they have English language or they have studied it separately but alongside the language. There is now a considerable resurgence of interest in the study of literature in relation to language. This book is designed to foster an integration of the study of English language and literature.

The aims and design of the book can be briefly summarised as follows: *The Web of Words* helps learners of English to understand and appreciate English literary texts. It does so by using a wide variety of learning techniques and exercises which often involve active group and pair work in class. The book focuses particularly on language where this is relevant to appreciate the style, effects and techniques of the writing. The main purpose is to help students to use response to language as a basis for reading and appreciating authentic literary sources.

We hope that such an integrated approach will stimulate students' language development and at the same time enhance sensitivity to the use of language in literature. We feel that this integrated approach is necessary even in mother-tongue English studies, although some native speakers can rely on their linguistic intuition and wide reading as a basis for the understanding of literature. With the non-native speaker, however, careful training is necessary. Our 'approaches' do not, of course, claim to deliver literary competence. They lay a basis of preliminary and pre-literary techniques and procedures which we hope will give students increasing confidence in their own understanding and appreciation. This 'preliminary and pre-literary' character requires a little explanation with reference to the kinds of student the book is aimed at, and the kinds of courses on which it can be used. In most cases students will probably be upper-intermediate or advanced. This will generally be a necessary prerequisite for the kind of language operations they are asked to perform.

1 Students may have previously followed courses in literature. It is unlikely that much explicit attention will have been given to writers' uses of language and style. This book is designed for use as the core component of the following types of course:
    - supplementary courses involving the intensive study of literary texts;
    - extension courses in literature where response to and awareness of language is an essential feature.

2 The book can also be used as an advanced language-based course book for students of literature whose primary course of study is language. Our view here is that an encounter with literary language should be an essential component of such study.

3 The 'preliminary and pre-literary' orientation of the book indicates our recognition that there is more to literature than just the language. Many factors, including historical, cultural and biographical aspects, as well as literary traditions, play a part in fuller reading and interpretation. Other course books do and will continue to illustrate this. *The Web of Words* is so designed that it can form the core of an integrated language and literature programme and that it can be used by teachers of both language and literature.

Teacher's Book

Teachers should know that there is an accompanying Teacher's Book for *The Web of Words*. It gives explicit guidance for using the book in the classroom and provides a fuller rationale than there is space for here. There are also detailed notes on each unit and on the uses of the approach connected with each unit, a range of further questions on selected texts, suggestions for combining the approaches on single texts, and biographical notes on the writers whose texts are studied in the book.

Fast route

Teachers with limited time or those who do not wish their students to study all the texts in all the units of the book may like to know that suggestions are given in the Teacher's Book for a 'fast route' through the book. This involves study of selected texts in each unit.

For the teacher and the student

Summary of the main principles and purposes of the book

1 *The Web of Words* offers a series of different approaches which are designed to assist students with an upper-intermediate level of English to encounter genuine

literary texts in English. The foundation for this is laid by activities and exercises which frequently involve work in pairs and small groups. Each approach is designed to help you to get closer to the text. This means that we give particular emphasis to the language of each text. Some units analyse language in more detail than others; but all the units aim to help you to appreciate how a text works and what its particular meanings are. Some of your work will be on parts of texts but the overall aim is to help you to work out what whole texts have to say to you.

2 We have tried to keep difficult linguistic terminology to a minimum. But there are places in the book where we examine writers' styles and in such units it is impossible to avoid some 'metalanguage' However, it is always more important to understand what the term describes than the precise term itself. Often the terminology helps us define language features easily and conveniently.

3 We hope that the book will help you to appreciate literary texts and at the same time increase your ability to read and write English. Some exercises are additionally designed to improve your language competence but all are directed to help you to enjoy reading a variety of literary texts in English. The exercises should help you to learn how to explain your responses with direct reference to features of the text.

4 We have selected texts from different periods of English literature. We would like to introduce you to a wide range of different writers and different kinds of text (in other words not just poetry, prose and drama but different types of poetry, prose and drama). Because our main emphasis is on language and style we feel it would be most practical to concentrate on modern texts. Students are in most cases studying language and literature, and their language can usually be best helped by contact with modern (that is, mostly twentieth-century) writing.

5 We have devoted one unit to the background of texts. The aim here is to show how texts relate to the contexts in which they were produced. This is a conventional but very valuable and necessary approach to literary study. It is impossible for us to cover everything but we should stress that our emphasis on language does not exclude other approaches. It is just that we consider that language study provides the most effective and necessary foundations.

6 It is important to understand that no one single approach can help you to understand a text. We hope that you will learn to apply different approaches or parts of them to different texts and to combine some of the approaches when you study a new text. To this end several of our texts recur or are 'recycled' in several different sections. The main aim of all our approaches and of the exercises which go with them is to involve you directly in the study of the text. This is why so many of the exercises ask you to write and talk about the texts in many different ways. We would like you to keep up this habit and become more confident in your responses to literary texts and gain more direct enjoyment from them.

7 Above all, we hope that the texts you study will be enjoyable and interesting, that they will stimulate your thoughts and feelings, and that the book will help you to discuss and write out your reactions in English. Our aim is to help you to learn to read literature in English carefully, confidently and with insight. If you

3

want to go on to read more literature after working through this introductory book, we will have been successful.

8 It is important to note that the units are designed to be worked through in sequence. Unit 10 involves more complex analysis than Unit 1, and the more 'linguistic' units occur towards the end of the book and are themselves progressively structured. But this is not a course book and it is, of course, open to those using the book to work through the units in an order appropriate to their needs. We have tried to ensure that each unit is sufficiently self-contained to allow this.

Unit 1 What's going on? Summary and narrative prediction

Introduction for the student

The purpose of this unit is to help you to write summaries of texts you have read and to make predictions while you read. These exercises are not designed to explain or interpret the text but they do provide you with a basis for understanding and becoming more involved in the text. It is important to note that these exercises are not a test and there will seldom be a completely correct answer. The exercises are best completed in groups or pairs.

SECTION A

Orientation

1 A useful preliminary exercise is to summarise material from newspapers. Select a main report from the front page of a newspaper (English or non-English) and reduce it to about one-third of its length. What have you left out? Why have you left it out? Have you altered the meaning of the report?

2 Reduce the length of this newspaper report by about one third.

Expert aims to salvage détente from ocean bed

ALAN ROAD reports on how an offer to help raise the sunken Soviet submarine could improve East-West relations.

IN an unprecedented venture in East-West co-operation, a private British marine salvage expert has offered his services to the Soviet Union in any attempt it makes to recover the wreck of its nuclear submarine which sank in the Atlantic last week.

The 10,000-ton Yankee-class, nuclear-powered ballistic missile submarine went down in 18,000ft of water while being towed to

a **Russian port after an**
explosion aboard, thought to
have been caused by a leak-
25 **age of rocket propellant.**
   Three crew members
were reported to have died
in the accident, which took
place about 1,000 miles off
the Eastern seaboard of the 30
United States.

The Observer

3 Is there any difference between the summary of a non-literary text and a literary text?

Summary I

1 Now read the following short story by Ernest Hemingway: 'Cat in the Rain'.

THERE were only two Americans stopping at the hotel. They did
not know any of the people they passed on the stairs on their way
to and from their room. Their room was on the second floor facing
the sea. It also faced the public garden and the war monument.
There were big palms and green benches in the public garden. In   5
the good weather there was always an artist with his easel. Artists
liked the way the palms grew and the bright colours of the hotels
facing the gardens and the sea. Italians came from a long way off
to look up at the war monument. It was made of bronze and
glistened in the rain. It was raining. The rain dripped from the   10
palm trees. Water stood in pools on the gravel paths. The sea
broke in a long line in the rain and slipped back down the beach to
come up and break again in a long line in the rain. The motor-cars
were gone from the square by the war monument. Across the
square in the doorway of the café a waiter stood looking out at the 15
empty square.
   The American wife stood at the window looking out. Outside
right under their window a cat was crouched under one of the
dripping green tables. The cat was trying to make herself so
compact that she would not be dripped on.   20
   'I'm going down and get that kitty,' the American wife said.
   'I'll do it,' her husband offered from the bed.
   'No, I'll get it. The poor kitty out trying to keep dry under a
table.'
   The husband went on reading, lying propped up with the two   25
pillows at the foot of the bed.
   'Don't get wet,' he said.
   The wife went downstairs and the hotel owner stood up and
bowed to her as she passed the office. His desk was at the far end
of the office. He was an old man and very tall.   30

6

'*Il piove*,' the wife said. She liked the hotel-keeper.

'*Si, si, Signora, brutto tempo*. It is very bad weather.'

He stood behind his desk in the far end of the dim room. The wife liked him. She liked the deadly serious way he received any complaints. She liked his dignity. She liked the way he wanted to serve her. She liked the way he felt about being a hotel-keeper. She liked his old, heavy face and big hands. 35

Liking him she opened the door and looked out. It was raining harder. A man in a rubber cape was crossing the empty square to the café. The cat would be around to the right. Perhaps she could go along under the eaves. As she stood in the doorway an umbrella opened behind her. It was the maid who looked after their room. 40

'You must not get wet,' she smiled, speaking Italian. Of course, the hotel-keeper had sent her. 45

With the maid holding the umbrella over her, she walked along the gravel path until she was under their window. The table was there, washed bright green in the rain, but the cat was gone. She was suddenly disappointed. The maid looked up at her.

'*Ha perduto qualque cosa, Signora?*' 50

'There was a cat,' said the American girl.

'A cat?'

'*Si, il gatto*.'

'A cat?' the maid laughed. 'A cat in the rain?'

'Yes,' she said, 'under the table.' Then, 'Oh, I wanted it so much. I wanted a kitty.' 55

When she talked English the maid's face tightened.

'Come, Signora,' she said. 'We must get back inside. You will be wet.'

'I suppose so,' said the American girl. 60

They went back along the gravel path and passed the door. The maid stayed outside to close the umbrella. As the American girl passed the office, the *padrone* bowed from his desk. Something felt very small and tight inside the girl. The *padrone* made her feel very small and at the same time really important. She had a momentary feeling of being of supreme importance. She went on up the stairs. She opened the door of the room. George was on the bed, reading. 65

'Did you get the cat?' he asked, putting the book down.

'It was gone.' 70

'Wonder where it went to?' he said, resting his eyes from reading.

She sat down on the bed.

'I wanted it so much,' she said. 'I don't know why I wanted it so much. I wanted that poor kitty. It isn't any fun to be a poor kitty out in the rain.' 75

[handwritten marginal notes: "disappointed?" (left margin); "kitten or baby? or love + affection. feels lonely" (right margin)]

7

George was reading again.

She went over and sat in front of the mirror of the dressing-table, looking at herself with the hand glass. She studied her profile, first one side and then the other. Then she studied the back of her head and her neck. 80

'Don't you think it would be a good idea if I let my hair grow out?' she asked, looking at her profile again.

George looked up and saw the back of her neck, clipped close like a boy's. 85

'I like it the way it is.'

bored

'I get so tired of it,' she said. 'I get so tired of looking like a boy.'

George shifted his position on the bed. He hadn't looked away from her since she started to speak.

'You look pretty darn nice,' he said. 90

She laid the mirror down on the dresser and went over to the window and looked out. It was getting dark.

I want, I want...
unfulfilled
life; describe
always want
things her way?
husband
loses patience

'I want to pull my hair back tight and smooth and make a big knot at the back that I can feel,' she said. 'I want to have a kitty to sit on my lap and purr when I stroke her.' 95

'Yeah?' George said from the bed.

'And I want to eat at a table with my own silver and I want candles. And I want it to be spring and I want to brush my hair out in front of a mirror and I want a kitty and I want some new clothes.' 100

'Oh, shut up and get something to read,' George said. He was reading again.

His wife was looking out of the window. It was quite dark now and still raining in the palm trees.

'Anyway, I want a cat,' she said. 'I want a cat. I want a cat now. 105 If I can't have long hair or any fun, I can have a cat.'

George was not listening. He was reading his book. His wife looked out of the window where the light had come on in the square.

Someone knocked at the door. 110

'*Avanti*,' George said. He looked up from his book.

In the doorway stood the maid. She held a big tortoiseshell cat pressed tight against her and swung down against her body.

'Excuse me,' she said, 'the *padrone* asked me to bring this for the Signora.' 115

domineering husband

Ernest Hemingway: 'Cat in the Rain'

2 Read the story a second time and, as you read it, underline the main points of the narrative. This should mean that you will underline about ten single words you think you will include in any summary of what happens in this story.

3 Now write a summary of what happens in 'Cat in the Rain' which includes the ten words you have already underlined. You should write your summary in approximately 50 words.

4 Compare summaries with another member of your group. What have you included and what have you left out in comparison with his or her summary?

5 Now write another summary of what happens in 'Cat in the Rain'. The rules this time are a little stricter:
   a) You must only use 25–30 words.
   b) You must not interpret the story. You must only summarise what happens in the narrative.
If you keep to 25–30 words you will really have to use language. It takes some skill to write a summary in an exact number of words. You may produce two or three drafts before you manage to get it right.

6 Here are three summaries. Work with another student and decide which one you like best and why. Consider, in particular, how far the rules in 5 have been followed:
   a) George's wife wants a cat in the rain. The hotel-keeper meets her and sees she is lonely and finds her cat.
   b) An American couple stay at a hotel. The wife wants a kitten. She cannot find it.
   c) A couple stay at a hotel. The wife sees a cat outside in the rain. She wants it but can't find it. The hotel-keeper sends her another cat.

7 Compare your own summaries with these and with the summaries of others in your group. What is common to each summary? The hotel? The cat? The kitten? The hotel-keeper? The husband (George)? The rain?

8 Work in pairs to decide what you think has to be left out in a summary of only 25–30 words. Which features of the narrative are the most important? *setting, characters, plot.*

9 Finally, does a summary of what happens in this story explain what the story is about? What do you think it is about? Is it, as the title suggests, about a cat in the rain? Which of the following would you choose as an alternative title?
   The Lonely American Wife
   An Unhappy Marriage
   The Hotel-keeper who Cares
Remember that each of these titles offers an interpretation. Hemingway does not seem to want to direct the reader. He prefers to let the reader make up his or her own mind. His title is perhaps selected because he wants the cat to stand for or symbolise something.

10 How is the title 'Cat in the Rain' different from the title 'Expert aims to salvage détente from ocean bed' (*Orientation*)? *matter-of-fact*

emotive

9

EXPLOITATION

Look at these pictures. Are they how you imagine the setting and the cat in the story?

Summary II

1 Here is a poem which presents an 'argument'. It is by the American poet Walt Whitman. On this occasion try to summarise the 'argument' in

10

about 30 words. In doing so, you may wish to consider the following questions:

a) Why did the poet become 'tired and sick' of listening to the astronomer?
b) Why did he go off by himself?
c) How did he see the sky and how different is his view from that of the astronomer?

> When I heard the learn'd astronomer,
> When the proofs, the figures, were ranged in columns before
>   me,
> When I was shown the charts and diagrams, to add, divide,
>   and measure them,
> When I sitting heard the astronomer where he lectured with
>   much applause in the lecture-room,
> How soon unaccountable I became tired and sick,   5
> Till rising and gliding out I wander'd off by myself,
> In the mystical moist night-air, and from time to time,
> Look'd up in perfect silence at the stars.

> Walt Whitman

2 What are the differences between what the poet actually says and your summary of the poem's argument?

3 Look at the following features of the poem:
a) the use of repetition for emphasis;
b) the long sentences;
c) The contrasts in word choice from one sentence to the other, e.g. sentence one: proofs, columns, figures; sentence two: mystical, moist, perfect, gliding.
What happens to these features in a summary of the poem?

EXPLOITATION AND SUMMARY OF SECTION A

1 Try to write more summaries of the literary texts you read. It gives a good basis for understanding the text.
2 Remember, though, that summarising 'plot' does not help account much for what a literary text means. When you read your summaries, try to see what you have left out and what you have not been able to summarise.
3 Try writing to within word limits. It gives good practice at handling the English language.
4 Summary is a technique we shall use throughout the book. You will get constant help with the activity.
5 Continue to examine why it is always easier to produce a summary of a non-literary text. Do we change the 'style' of a non-literary text when we summarise it? What about a literary text?
6 You may like to know that 'Cat in the Rain' is studied further in Unit 10, page 175.

SECTION B

Orientation

1 When we read we have an expectation of what will follow. We predict, with a reasonable degree of certainty, the following word or words, and, with less certainty, the following paragraph, pages, and so on. This means that when we are in the middle of any piece of text, our mind refers back to what we have already read, and projects forward to what we are about to read. Without prediction the reader would lack orientation and reading would be more difficult. Prediction and reading fluency are therefore inseparable.

   When we predict the following word or words the process is partly linguistic and partly involves our 'knowledge of the world'. Suppose you open an air letter sheet, but cut it in such a way that one line can no longer be read. You can read, on the last line before the unfortunate cut:

I am just recovering from a bad

What word do you expect to follow?
   accident   night   cold   debt   omen

Each of these nouns 'collocates' (fits together) with the adjective 'bad'. In the absence of any other information in the letter which might be important:
a) Which noun would you choose?
b) How does the word 'recovering' affect your choice?
c) Do you think the process of selecting the word is linguistic, or involves knowledge of the world, or both?

2 Let us take this process a step further. Imagine this extract is from a popular novel. Predict what follows:
   'As he got near the airport Leonard checked his briefcase for the fifth time to make sure he had got .... ,

   Continue with the following, from an imaginary simple science text ('knowledge of the world' is necessary here):
   'It is extremely dangerous to stand in water when you turn on ....
   This is because .... ,

   or from a 'serious' or philosophical text:
   'No religious person doubts .... ,

3 Look at this picture.

The first words of the caption are:
> *A Cambridge taxi driver was . . .*

What do you predict follows?

The caption continues:
> *A Cambridge taxi driver was crushed*
> *to death when . . .*

What do you now predict? The complete caption, which is taken from a
Cambridge newspaper, is printed upside down at the bottom of the page.

Prediction I

When we read literature we predict in precisely the same way, though we probably
extend the *short-term prediction* of the preceding examples, especially in narrative,
to 'what follows in the next few paragraphs' (which we shall call *intermediate-term
prediction*) or 'what follows in the next few chapters', or 'the remainder of the
story or book' (*long-term prediction*).

> *A Cambridge taxi driver was crushed*
> *to death when a 1,000-ton goods train*
> *ploughed into his car on an unmanned*
> *level crossing.*

1 We begin with a short-term and relatively easy prediction from *The Secret Agent* by Joseph Conrad. Read the following paragraph. Predict in one sentence what follows.

> She started forward at once, as if she were still a loyal woman bound to that man by an unbroken contract. Her right hand skimmed slightly the end of the table, and when she had passed on towards the sofa the carving knife had vanished without the slightest sound from the side of the dish. Mr. Verloc heard the 5 creaky plank in the floor, and was content. He waited. Mrs. Verloc was coming. As if the homeless soul of Stevie had flown for shelter straight to the breast of his sister, guardian, and protector, the resemblance of her face with that of her brother grew at every step, even to the droop of the lower lip, even to the 10 slight divergence of the eyes. But Mr. Verloc did not see that. He was lying on his back and staring upwards. He saw partly on the ceiling and partly on the wall the moving shadow of an arm with a clenched hand holding a carving knife. It flickered up and down. Its movements were leisurely. They were leisurely enough for 15 Mr. Verloc to recognise the limb and the weapon.

> Joseph Conrad: *The Secret Agent*

(See *Appendix 1* for the following paragraph.)

2 Suggest what could have happened between Mr Verloc and Stevie to justify your prediction of Mrs Verloc's action. (*Note:* This is not prediction, but an explanation of what has already happened, and is known to anyone who has read the book to this point.)

Prediction II

1 Read the following extract, which is from *The History of Mr. Polly,* by H. G. Wells (published 1910).

> And now Mr. Polly began to lead a double life. With the Johnsons he professed to be inclined, but not so conclusively inclined as to be inconvenient, to get a shop for himself—to be, to use the phrase he preferred, "looking for an opening." He would ride off in the afternoon upon that research, remarking that he was 5 going to "cast a strategical eye" on Chertsey or Weybridge. But if not all roads, still a great majority of them led by however devious ways to Stamton, and to laughter and increasing familiarity. Relations developed with Annie and Minnie and Miriam. Their various characters were increasingly interesting. The laughter 10 became perceptibly less abundant, something of the fizz had gone from the first opening, still these visits remained wonderfully

friendly and upholding. Then back he would come to grave but evasive discussions with Johnson.

Johnson was really anxious to get Mr. Polly "into something." 15
His was a reserved, honest character, and he would really have preferred to see his lodger doing things for himself than receive his money for house-keeping. He hated waste, anybody's waste, much more than he desired profit. But Mrs. Johnson was all for Mr. Polly's loitering. She seemed much the more human and likeable 20
of the two to Mr. Polly.

He tried at times to work up enthusiasm for the various avenues to well-being his discussion with Johnson opened. But they remained disheartening prospects. He imagined himself wonderfully smartened up, acquiring style and value in a London shop; 25
but the picture was stiff and unconvincing. He tried to rouse himself to enthusiasm by the idea of his property increasing by leaps and bounds, by twenty pounds a year or so, let us say, each year, in a well-placed little shop, the corner shop Johnson favoured. There was a certain picturesque interest in imagining 30
cut-throat economics, but his heart told him there would be little in practising them.

And then it happened to Mr. Polly that real Romance came out of dreamland into his life, intoxicated and gladdened him with sweetly beautiful suggestions—and left him. She came and left 35
him as that dear lady leaves so many of us, alas! not sparing him one jot or one tittle of the hollowness of her retreating aspect.

It was all the more to Mr. Polly's taste that the thing should happen as things happen in books.

In a resolute attempt not to get to Stamton that day, he had 40
turned due southward from Easewood towards a country where the abundance of bracken jungles, lady's smock, stitchwort, bluebells, and grassy stretches by the wayside under shady trees does much to compensate the lighter type of mind for the absence of promising "openings." He turned aside from the road, wheeled his machine 45
along a faintly marked attractive trail through bracken until he came to a heap of logs against a high old stone wall with a damaged coping and wallflower plants already gone to seed. He sat down, balanced the straw hat on a convenient lump of wood, lit a cigarette, and abandoned himself to agreeable musings and the 50
friendly observation of a cheerful little brown and gray bird his stillness presently encouraged to approach him.

"This is All Right," said Mr. Polly softly to the little brown and gray bird. "Business—later."

He reflected that he might go on this way for four or five years, 55
and then be scarcely worse off than he had been in his father's lifetime.

"Vile Business," said Mr. Polly.

Then Romance appeared. Or to be exact, Romance became audible. 60

Romance began as a series of small but increasingly vigorous movements on the other side of the wall, then a voice murmuring, then as a falling of little fragments on the other side and as ten pink finger-tips, scarcely apprehended before Romance became start-lingly and emphatically a leg, remained for a time a fine, slender, 65 actively struggling limb, brown stockinged, and wearing a brown toe-worn shoe, and then. . . . A handsome, red-haired girl wearing a short dress of blue linen was sitting astride the wall, panting, considerably disarranged by her climbing, and as yet unaware of Mr. Polly. . . . 70

H. G. Wells: *The History of Mr. Polly*

2 So Mr Polly meets a 'handsome red-haired girl wearing a short dress of blue linen'. Consider first Mr Polly's character. Note the words 'evasive' and 'dreamland' in the text, and see if there are any other pointers to the sort of person Mr Polly is. Then working in groups predict in two or three sentences the immediate progress of Mr Polly's 'Romance' (bearing in mind that the novel was first published in 1910).

3 When you are in agreement on an intermediate-term prediction, we should like to point out that 'what follows' is a dialogue. Use your prediction to try and reconstruct this dialogue. Then read *Appendix 2*.

EXPLOITATION

In this section we return to Hemingway's story 'Cat in the Rain' (see *Summary I*). You are invited to make a long-term prediction. Read the story again and write two paragraphs describing how you think the action will develop beyond the 'end' of the story as supplied by Hemingway. Ask yourself:
a) Will the relationship between 'the American couple' remain the same?
b) Will the wife recognise that the hotel-keeper has responded to her needs and thus develop a relationship with him?
c) Will the wife consider that the hotel-keeper has just sent up '*a* cat' not '*the* cat' she was searching for and thus feel that no-one really understands her?
d) What is there in the story as told by Hemingway which enables us to predict an outcome to the situation?
e) Why does the story end where it does?

Prediction III

1 One group of poems which are always brought to a resolution are the Elizabethan sonnets. These sonnets are often very complex, but once the reader becomes familiar with the thematic progression, it becomes possible to predict

the outcome. The example which follows is an early sonnet by Edmund Spenser (1552–99).*

> Of this world's Theatre in which we stay,
>   my love lyke the Spectator ydly sits
>   beholding me that all the pageants play,
>   disguysing diversly my troubled wits.
> Sometimes I joy when glad occasion fits,   5
>   and mask in myrth lyke to a Comedy:
>   soone after when my joy to sorrow flits,
>   I waile and make my woes a Tragedy.
> Yet she beholding me with constant eye,
>   delights not in my merth nor rues my smart: 10
>   but when I laugh she mocks, and when I cry
>   she laughes, and hardens evermore her hart.

Edmund Spenser

The poem is an extended simile. The outlines of a summary may help.
   'My beloved is like a spectator watching me act on the stage. Sometimes I play comic parts and sometimes tragic parts. The only trouble is that when I play comic roles she just mocks me, and laughs outright at my tragic parts . . .'

So how is this resolved in the last two lines?
Extend this list of suggestions:
a) It seems I lose whatever I do.
b) Perhaps, I should ask her to share my comic or tragic mood.
c) Such a woman can never understand true feelings.
d) ....
e) ....
f) ....

2 Work with another student to extend the above list. Then meet in groups and decide on the sentence which you think resolves the poem most satisfactorily.
   Look up the original final couplet in *Appendix 3* and compare it with your prediction.
   Note: Obviously you cannot expect to guess the poet's exact words, so it is sufficient that you and your partner should agree that your resolution is reasonable and you find it satisfactory. It is then interesting to compare your resolution with the idea, and the actual words, of the original.

Prediction IV

The final poem in this section is by A. E. Housman (1859–1936). The poem is a dialogue between a young man who has died and his friend or peer who is still

---

* This poem is studied again in Unit 6, *Vocabulary IV*, with reference to its structure and vocabulary; it is printed in that unit in modern spelling.

alive. There is evidence for believing the friend is still young. Each question by the dead man elicits a precise answer in the following stanza. The dead man asks questions about his life style, and village, and acquaintances. He wants to know, basically, if things are as they were. Thus:

> 'Is my team ploughing,
>   That I was used to drive
> And hear the harness jingle
>   When I was man alive?'

Death is, in one aspect, a fear of the unknown. The news that things here, in life, are anyway unchanged might be reassuring to the dead man. It is just this reassurance that the second speaker provides in his response:

> Ay, the horses trample,   5
>   The harness jingles now;
> No change though you lie under
>   The land you used to plough.

Note 'no change' in line 3. This, so far, is the substance of the answer. Here then is the next question from the dead man, a slightly unusual one to find in poetry, asking about football:

> 'Is football playing
>   Along the river shore,   10
> With lads to chase the leather,
>   Now I stand up no more?'

The answer is again, in effect, 'no change':

> Ay, the ball is flying,
>   The lads play heart and soul,
> The goal stands up, the keeper   15
>   Stands up to keep the goal.

The poem takes on a more intimate character in the next question, and this is perhaps the question the dead man really wanted to ask, and for which football was only a 'lead in':

> 'Is my girl happy,
>   That I thought hard to leave,
> And has she tired of weeping
>   As she lies down at eve?'   20

The answer is again one of reassurance:

> Ay, she lies down lightly,
>   She lies not down to weep:
> Your girl is well contented.
>   Be still, my lad, and sleep

It is possible that there are clues in the above stanza to the final resolution. For instance how can the second speaker be so sure that:

> 'Your girl is well contented'?

Note that he shows some loss of patience, even irritation, when he says 'Be still, my lad'. But he does not discourage the persistent questioning:

> 'Is my friend hearty,   25
>   Now I am thin and pine,
> And has he found to sleep in
>   A better bed than mine?'

Consider, first, if the question is literally about a bed. This is the last question. How is the poem resolved? Is it 'no change' as in stanzas 2, 4 and 6? Or do you predict a change, and if so, what?

Decide on an individual answer and write it down in one or two sentences. Discuss these answers in groups and reach consensus before checking the poet's resolution in the final stanza in *Appendix 4*.

SUMMARY OF SECTION B

1 Prediction is a different activity from summarising. Not having the whole text in front of them, readers cannot make a summary of it; however, they do make mental summaries of what they have read and use this as a basis to predict what will happen.
2 We predict and anticipate most strongly what will happen next when the text has a clear plot–narrative line.
3 Continue to project your mind forward when you read, comparing your predictions with those of others in your group. A most suitable story for both short- and long-term prediction is 'The Force of Circumstance' in Unit 10.

Unit 2   Scenario: Language, dialogue and setting

Introduction for the student

In this unit we want you to imagine you are making a film or videotape of a text or are the director of a play. You are also the producer and have as wide a choice as you need of actors, actresses, resources for costume, lighting and make-up. You may also choose any setting you want, outside or inside.

Our aim here is to help you to explore some of the 'pictures' created by the language of a text. You examine the relationship between language and other media.

You should try to make the written text 'come alive' in this different medium but this can only be done by examining the text carefully and by working out what it means to you. Group work is essential to this unit. Directors and producers have to take individual decisions but they are also part of a team. In the next section a sample of the technique is worked out in detail.

Our aim here is to help you to explore some of the 'pictures' created by the language of a text. You examine the relationship between language and other media.

Orientation

1   Read the following poem carefully.

Meeting at Night

The grey sea and the long black land;
And the yellow half-moon large and low;
And the startled little waves that leap
In fiery ringlets from their sleep,
As I gain the cove with pushing prow,   5
And quench its speed i' the slushy sand.

Then a mile of warm sea-scented beach;
Three fields to cross till a farm appears;
A tap at the pane, the quick sharp scratch
And blue spurt of a lighted match,   10
And a voice less loud, thro' its joys and fears,
Than the two hearts beating each to each!

Robert Browning

20

2 You are required to produce a 'visual' in the form of a videotape to accompany the above poem. The tape will last only a few minutes, but note that it will be considerably longer than the time it takes to read the poem.

Scenario as follows:

Introduction: Speaker sitting at desk in a study with bookshelves behind. Single book open on desk in front of the speaker.

'Today's poem is called "Meeting at Night" by Robert Browning. Browning was an English poet who was born in 1812 and died in 1889.'

– insert still picture of Browning –

'His life thus covered much of the Victorian period, and his many poems' . . .

– insert title page of *The Poems of Robert Browning* –

. . . 'capture some of the atmosphere of Victorian England. This poem is short, only twelve lines, but it has a powerful visual element in the words.'

Second Speaker:

The grey sea . . .	A dark bay, hills in the background. Some movement of the sea, but generally calm.
and the long black land	Camera moves out to picture sea only. Moon low over horizon, heavy clouds momentarily moving across.
And the yellow half-moon large and low	Camera moves in to shore, small waves breaking on the beach.

Time used: 1 minute

- -

And the startled little waves that leap (pause)	Moonlight only, hills in background very dark.
In fiery ringlets from their sleep	Rowing boat comes into view, coming towards beach. Close-up of rower: Man, aged .... ? Dress .... ?
As I gain the cove	Boat comes closer and closer to the camera, bows first, so that only the back of the rower is visible.
with pushing prow	Boat drives hard into the sand of the beach. Sound effects .... ?

⟫→

21

And quench its speed i' the slushy sand	Boat stops. Man jumps up, stumbles, runs a few paces, then moves quickly up the beach, head down.
	Camera focuses on empty boat on the beach, oars still in the water.

Total time elapsed:
.... minutes

	Fade.

	Fade in.
Then a mile of warm sea-scented beach	Man now walking quickly across a field. Still near total darkness but close-up of man's face. Age now clearly about .... ?
	Continues walking quickly, crouching slightly. Stops once to listen, look around.
Three fields to cross till a farm appears	Outline of farm buildings. Sound effects .... ?
A tap at the pane	Man tiptoes last few steps to a downstairs window, taps, waits.
	– 10-second pause, silence.
the quick sharp scratch	– sound effect.
And blue spurt of a lighted match	Girl's face, very close to *inside* of window, lit by the flare of a lighted match.
	Then darkness
And a voice less loud, thro' its joys and fears	Woman calls out a man's name. Name .... ? Voice, manner of call .... ?
(pause)	
Than the two hearts beating each to each!	Camera moves to close-up of man's face, which breaks into a smile.
	Arm movements of both man and girl .... ?
	Fade to: Reader at desk as at beginning.

Total time elapsed:
.... minutes

22

Discuss briefly each of the blanks where there is a question mark, and decide on an appropriate answer.

Scenario I

1 We would now like you to devise a 'scenario' as in *Orientation* above for Shelley's well-known poem 'Ozymandias' (see also Unit 3, *Orientation*).

Ozymandias

I MET a traveller from an antique land
Who said: Two vast and trunkless legs of stone
Stand in the desert . . . Near them, on the sand,
Half sunk, a shattered visage lies, whose frown,
And wrinkled lip, and sneer of cold command,   5
Tell that its sculptor well those passions read
Which yet survive, stamped on these lifeless things,
The hand that mocked them, and the heart that fed:
And on the pedestal these words appear:
'My name is Ozymandias, king of kings: 10
Look on my works, ye Mighty, and despair!'
Nothing beside remains. Round the decay
Of that colossal wreck, boundless and bare
The lone and level sands stretch far away.

Percy Bysshe Shelley

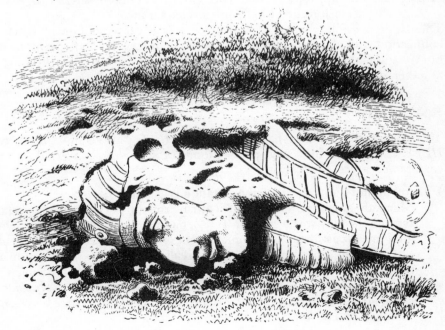

2 You are required to produce a 'visual' on videotape for this poem, 'on location'. Write a programme as in 1 above, detailing the introduction, setting, lighting, the representation of the words on the pedestal (voice-over?) etc. Focus particularly on the traveller, who should also be the narrator or 'voice' from line 2:

> 'Two vast and trunkless legs of stone'

Decide how to present the opening line. Who is the speaker? Where is he, and the traveller? Remember to project the appearance of an early nineteenth-century traveller. Estimate the total time of your visual.

EXPLOITATION

Work in groups for this exercise. This is an exercise in adapting a literary text to a modern setting. This is relatively common, one example being the movie *Apocalypse Now* (1980) which draws on Joseph Conrad's novel *Heart of Darkness*.

You are required to make a 'modern adaptation' for a short videotape of about ten minutes (you must estimate the time distribution/breakdown) based on Shelley's poem 'Ozymandias'.

a) Imagine that 'the traveller' is the survivor of a nuclear attack on any city in Western Europe.
b) The 'statue' is then the remains of that city, which you would show with suitable visual material.
c) Find an appropriate comparison for 'these words' in line 9 of the poem.
d) Work out all other suitable comparisons.
e) Decide on the appropriate visual presentation of line 14:

> 'The lone and level sands stretch far away'

There is no possible 'correct' answer to (b). It is an exercise of the imagination in connection with a literary text. Do not write your scenarios (cf. *Orientation* above) but try and make as many comparisons as possible with the poem, keeping in mind as a theme 'Nothing beside remains' (line 12).

Scenario II

This extract is from Shakespeare's play *Macbeth*. (See also Unit 4, *Reading aloud III*.) The scenario is for a stage production, so you have no concern this time with camera or features of location.

1 If you do not know the play, the situation is as follows:
   Macbeth, a senior officer in the Scottish army (in perhaps an 11th century setting; the play was written in 1606), has just murdered the King, who was a guest in his castle. In this complete scene (Act II Scene 2) Macbeth could be said to be suffering from shock, as he realises the horror of his action and the possible consequences. The purpose of his action is to become King himself. Lady Macbeth, a forceful and ambitious woman, attempts to set aside her husband's fears and doubts. It is night, presumably sometime between midnight and dawn.

2 Work in pairs. Decide on suitable ways of staging this scene. Each of the notes in the right-hand margin is intended as a question. Thus 'Lighting?' means 'What lighting would you use at this point for a stage production?'

It is suggested that you make pencil notes in the margin after:

a) reading the text;

b) discussing each point with your partner.

You may of course make additional notes for a production if you wish; that is, notes for lines where there is no question.

Enter Lady Macbeth	a) Position on stage?
LADY	
That which hath made them drunk hath made me bold;	b) Looking in which direction?
What hath quenched them hath given me fire. – Hark! – Peace!	
It was the owl that shrieked, the fatal bellman	c) Head movement?
Which gives the stern'st good-night. He is about it.	
5 The doors are open, and the surfeited grooms	d) Lighting?
Do mock their charges with snores; I have drugged their possets	
That death and nature do contend about them	
Whether they live or die.	
MACBETH (*within*) Who's there? What, ho!	e) Voice – distant or near?
LADY	
Alack, I am afraid they have awaked,	f) Pause (if any)?
10 And 'tis not done. The attempt and not the deed	
Confounds us. – Hark! – I laid their daggers ready;	
He could not miss 'em. Had he not resembled	
My father as he slept, I had done't.	
Enter Macbeth, carrying two bloodstained daggers	
My husband!	
MACBETH	g) Manner of entry?
I have done the deed. Didst thou not hear a noise?	
LADY	
15 I heard the owl-scream and the cricket's cry.	
Did you not speak?	
MACBETH When?	
LADY Now.	
MACBETH As I descended?	
LADY	
Ay.	
MACBETH	
Hark!	
Who lies i'the second chamber?	
LADY Donalbain.	

25

MACBETH (*looks at his hands*)
20   This is a sorry sight.

LADY
A foolish thought, to say a sorry sight.

MACBETH
There's one did laugh in's sleep, and one cried 'Murder!'
That they did wake each other. I stood and heard them

But they did say their prayers and addressed them
25   Again to sleep.

LADY   There are two lodged together.

MACBETH
One cried 'God bless us' and 'Amen' the other,
As they had seen me with these hangman's hands.
Listening their fear I could not say 'Amen'
When they did say 'God bless us.'

LADY
30   Consider it not so deeply.

MACBETH
But wherefore could not I pronounce 'Amen'?
I had most need of blessing, and 'Amen'
Stuck in my throat.

LADY   These deeds must not be thought
After these ways; so, it will make us mad.

MACBETH
35   Methought I heard a voice cry, 'Sleep no more!
Macbeth does murder sleep – the innocent sleep,
Sleep that knits up the ravelled sleave of care,
The death of each day's life, sore labour's bath,
Balm of hurt minds, great nature's second course,
40   Chief nourisher in life's feast.'

LADY   What do you mean?

MACBETH
Still it cried 'Sleep no more' to all the house;
'Glamis hath murdered sleep, and therefore Cawdor
Shall sleep no more, Macbeth shall sleep no more.'

LADY
Who was it that thus cried? Why, worthy thane,
45   You do unbend your noble strength, to think
So brain-sickly of things. Go, get some water,
And wash this filthy witness from your hand.
Why did you bring these daggers from the
        place?
They must lie there. Go, carry them and smear
50   The sleepy grooms with blood.

h) Arm or body movement? Lighting? Spotlight?
i) Looking in which direction?
j) Movement(s) (if any)?

k) Arm movements?

l) Manner of speaking?

m) Eye movement during this speech:
– to the audience?
– to Lady Macbeth?
– other possibilities?

n) Lady Macbeth's manner of indicating 'your hand'?

26

MACBETH   I'll go no more.
I am afraid to think what I have done;
Look on't again I dare not.

LADY   Infirm of purpose!
Give me the daggers. The sleeping and the dead
Are but as pictures. 'Tis the eye of childhood
55   That fears a painted devil. If he do bleed,
I'll gild the faces of the grooms withal,
For it must seem their guilt.   *Exit*
    Knock within

MACBETH   Whence is that knocking?
How is't with me when every noise appals me?
What hands are here! Ha – they pluck out mine eyes!
60   Will all great Neptune's ocean wash this blood
Clean from my hand? No, this my hand will rather
The multitudinous seas incarnadine,
Making the green one red.
    Enter Lady Macbeth

LADY
My hands are of your colour; but I shame
65   To wear a heart so white.
    Knock
                          I hear a knocking
At the south entry. Retire we to our chamber.
A little water clears us of this deed;
How easy it is then! Your constancy
Hath left you unattended.
    Knock
                          Hark! more knocking.
70   Get on your nightgown, lest occasion call us
And show us to be watchers. Be not lost
So poorly in your thoughts.

MACBETH
To know my deed 'twere best not know myself.
    Knock
Wake Duncan with thy knocking! I would thou couldst!
                          Exeunt

o)	Arm movement?
p)	Sound effect?
q)	Pause (if any)?
r)	Change of lighting (if on)?
s)	Manner of entry?
t)	Movements of both characters?
u)	Pause? Action during pause?
v)	Action to accompany the word 'Hark'?
w)	Speaking to whom?
x)	Leave stage together/ separately?
y)	Final lighting?

William Shakespeare: *Macbeth* (II, ii)

Scenario III

1 This is a very short but complete play called *Last to Go* by the modern British playwright Harold Pinter (born 1930). Like Act II Scene 2 of *Macbeth* there are only two people involved, though in this case both are men. Another common feature with the *Macbeth* text is that it is certainly night. We can deduce this from a minor cross-cultural point. One of the characters, 'an old newspaper seller' refers to the *Evening News* and *The Standard*, which are (or were at the time the play was written) London evening newspapers.

   Thereafter we note only differences between Act II Scene 2 of *Macbeth* and *Last to Go*. You must decide how these differences affect the scenario. Look in particular at *Last to Go* and decide which aspects of it go against many of the popular ideas of what constitutes a 'play'. Consider in particular:
   a) the kind of 'action' on stage;
   b) the nature of the language used;
   c) the social station of the characters.

2 Here is the preface and the first five lines of *Last to Go*:

   > *A coffee stall. A* BARMAN *and an old* NEWSPAPER SELLER.
   > *The* BARMAN *leans on his counter, the* OLD MAN *stands with tea. Silence.*

MAN	You was a bit busier earlier.
BARMAN	Ah.
MAN	Round about ten.
BARMAN	Ten, was it?
MAN	About then.
	Pause.

   Now work in groups for all activities connected with this text.
   You have a limited range of 'stage instructions' as, for example 'A coffee stall' and 'The barman leans . . .', 'the old man stands . . .'. These must be observed. But consider the following points and suggest tentative answers. You may modify these when you have read the whole play, if you think it is necessary.
   a) Where on the stage is the 'coffee stall'?
      (left, right, centre, front, back)
   b) What age (about) is (i) the barman, (ii) the newspaper seller?
   c) What kind of clothes are they wearing?
      (smart, shabby; suitable for winter or summer)
   d) What 'props' are on stage, if any? How is the coffee stall equipped?
   e) How close are the two characters to each other?
   f) Do they look at each other as they speak?
      Where do they look?
   g) How long are the pauses between each response?
      Are they all the same length?
   h) What is the lighting for (i) the coffee stall, (ii) the rest of the stage?

i)   What is the backdrop, behind the coffee stall, if any?
j)   Does either of the characters move during these five lines? If so, to where, or which part of their body do they move?

All the above questions are directly connected with your scenario. Write your answers in note form. But consider also (in your group) the following questions, and at an appropriate time, perhaps after the completion of the scenario, compare your answers with other groups.

Questions:
Not only is there little action; there is very little thought. But is there communication?
Do you think the two characters are happy to converse in this way?
Would they be happy with more 'content'?
If so what are they likely to talk about?
And, finally, what motivates the two men to continue their fragmented conversation?

3   Here is the remainder of the play. Continue in your groups and prepare your scenario for the whole, noting all movements, lighting changes, significant voice changes etc. Use the questions from 2 above as your guide, but do not restrict yourself to these. Write your comments in note form in pencil beside the text, if this is possible. (This is common practice among theatre producers, who may cover the page in notes!)
     Pay close attention to the word '*Pause*' which is important in the work of Pinter. Decide how many seconds to give each pause, and consider the impact of a longer pause on each occasion.

MAN	I passed by here about then.	
BARMAN	Oh yes?	
MAN	I noticed you were doing a bit of trade.	
	Pause.	
BARMAN	Yes, trade was very brisk here about ten.	
MAN	Yes, I noticed.	5
	Pause.	
	I sold my last one about then. Yes. About nine forty-five.	
BARMAN	Sold your last then, did you?	
MAN	Yes, my last 'Evening News' it was. Went about twenty to ten.	10
	Pause.	
BARMAN	'Evening News', was it?	
MAN	Yes.	
	Pause.	
	Sometimes it's the 'Star' is the last to go.	
BARMAN	Ah.	
MAN	Or the . . . whatsisname.	15

BARMAN   'Standard'.
MAN   Yes.   20
             Pause.
             All I had left tonight was the 'Evening News'.
             Pause.
BARMAN   Then that went, did it?
MAN   Yes.
             Pause.
             Like a shot.
             Pause.
BARMAN   You didn't have any left, eh?
MAN   No. Not after I sold that one.
             Pause.
BARMAN   It was after that you must have come by here then,
             was it?   25
MAN   Yes, I come by here after that, see, after I packed up.
BARMAN   You didn't stop here though, did you?
MAN   When?
BARMAN   I mean, you didn't stop here and have a cup of tea
             then, did you?   30
MAN   What, about ten?
BARMAN   Yes.
MAN   No, I went up to Victoria.*
BARMAN   No, I thought I didn't see you.
MAN   I had to go up to Victoria.   35
             Pause.
BARMAN   Yes, trade was very brisk here about then.
             Pause.
MAN   I went to see if I could get hold of George.
BARMAN   Who?
MAN   George.
             Pause.
BARMAN   George who?   40
MAN   George . . . whatsisname.
BARMAN   Oh.
             Pause.
             Did you get hold of him?
MAN   No. No, I couldn't get hold of him. I couldn't locate
             him.   45
BARMAN   He's not much about now, is he?
             Pause.
MAN   When did you last see him then?
BARMAN   Oh, I haven't seen him for years.

---

* Victoria – a district, and an important railway station, in London.

MAN	No, nor me.	
	Pause.	
BARMAN	Used to suffer very bad from arthritis.	50
MAN	Arthritis?	
BARMAN	Yes.	
MAN	He never suffered from arthritis.	
BARMAN	Suffered very bad.	
	Pause.	
MAN	Not when I knew him.	55
	Pause.	
BARMAN	I think he must have left the area.	
	Pause.	
MAN	Yes, it was the 'Evening News' was the last to go tonight.	
BARMAN	Not always the last though, is it, though?	
MAN	No. Oh no. I mean sometimes it's the 'News'. Other times it's one of the others. No way of telling beforehand. Until you've got your last one left, of course. Then you can tell which one it's going to be.	60
BARMAN	Yes.	65
	Pause.	
MAN	Oh yes.	
	Pause.	
	I think he must have left the area.	

Harold Pinter: *Last to Go*

4 When you have completed your scenario for *III* go back to the first five lines and see if you wish to make any changes in your answers to the ten questions in number 2. Remember that a theatre producer makes many changes as the rehearsal proceeds, until he or she 'gets it right'.

5 Do you consider the last line:
        'I think he must have left the area'
a) a completion?
b) a climax?
c) an anticlimax?
Give your reasons and compare with other groups.

6 Number 1 above mentioned two differences between Act II Scene 2 of *Macbeth* and *Last to Go* as drama. Of course this does not refer to differences in the plot or 'story'.

⟫→

31

The differences already noted are:

	Macbeth II, ii	*Last to Go*
a)	The participants in the drama are important people.	The participants in the drama are socially or politically *un*important.
b)	High level of conflict, or emotion, between participants.	Low level of conflict, or emotion, between participants.

A third difference is immediately noted in the first line of each text:

Macbeth   'That which hath made them drunk hath made me bold'
          (poetic line, ten syllables, regular stress)
Last to Go 'You was a bit busier earlier'
          (non-standard dialect)

Extend this list of differences noting as many points as possible in which these texts (*Macbeth* and *Last to Go*) are different both as drama, and in style.
Note: Your list here could be very extensive.

Scenario IV

The text of this section is Chapter 1 of *Great Expectations* by Charles Dickens. Your task is to prepare a scenario for making it into a film. The setting is England, about 1850. The text is accompanied by a picture (see below), as was common in 19th century novels. The picture has a caption,
       'The Terrible Stranger in the Churchyard'
which gives a clue to what is to follow in the text. The caption, in fact, employs two techniques closely related to those used in Unit 1 of this book. First it summarises the scene and acts as a stimulus to read the text. So:
       Somebody meets a terrible stranger in a churchyard
(the addition of a verb completes the sense of the caption). As there are two characters in the picture, and it is not difficult to decide which is 'the terrible stranger', we see immediately that the other is a boy. We are then able to expand our summary to:
       A boy meets a terrible stranger in a churchyard.
By a little elaboration (small boy? big boy?) we are able to make a fairly complete summary without having read a word. Look at the picture.

The Terrible Stranger in the Churchyard

The second of our 'approaches' from Unit 1, Prediction, is also relevant here. The caption which we have constructed above ('A small boy meets a terrible stranger in a churchyard') leads on logically to the question: 'And what happens?'
In preparing a scenario you will find both these techniques useful.

1   The text which follows is for adaptation as cinema film, without a narrator.
    Read the following passage carefully.

> MY father's family name being Pirrip, and my christian name
> Philip, my infant tongue could make of both names nothing
> longer or more explicit than Pip. So I called myself Pip, and came
> to be called Pip.
>   I give Pirrip as my father's family name, on the authority of his   5
> tombstone and my sister—Mrs. Joe Gargery, who married the
> blacksmith. As I never saw my father or my mother, and never saw
> any likeness of either of them (for their days were long before the
> days of photographs), my first fancies regarding what they were
> like, were unreasonably derived from their tombstones. The shape   10
> of the letters on my father's, gave me an odd idea that he was a
> square, stout, dark man, with curly black hair. From the character

33

and turn of the inscription, '*Also Georgiana Wife of the Above,*' I
drew a childish conclusion that my mother was freckled and
sickly. To five little stone lozenges, each about a foot and a half 15
long, which were arranged in a neat row beside their grave, and
were sacred to the memory of five little brothers of mine—who
gave up trying to get a living exceedingly early in that universal
struggle—I am indebted for a belief I religiously entertained that
they had all been born on their backs with their hands in their 20
trousers-pockets, and had never taken them out in this state of
existence.

Ours was the marsh country, down by the river, within, as the
river wound, twenty miles of the sea. My first most vivid and broad
impression of the identity of things, seems to me to have been 25
gained on a memorable raw afternoon towards evening. At such a
time I found out for certain, that this bleak place overgrown with
nettles was the churchyard; and that Philip Pirrip, late of this
parish, and also Georgiana wife of the above, were dead and
buried; and that Alexander, Bartholomew, Abraham, Tobias, 30
and Roger, infant children of the aforesaid, were also dead and
buried; and that the dark flat wilderness beyond the churchyard,
intersected with dykes and mounds and gates, with scattered cattle
feeding on it, was the marshes; and that the low leaden line
beyond was the river; and that the distant savage lair from which 35
the wind was rushing, was the sea; and that the small bundle of
shivers growing afraid of it all and beginning to cry, was Pip.

'Hold your noise!' cried a terrible voice, as a man started up
from among the graves at the side of the church porch. 'Keep still,
you little devil, or I'll cut your throat!' 40

A fearful man, all in coarse grey, with a great iron on his leg. A
man with no hat, and with broken shoes, and with an old rag tied
round his head. A man who had been soaked in water, and
smothered in mud, and lamed by stones, and cut by flints, and
stung by nettles, and torn by briars; who limped and shivered, and 45
glared and growled; and whose teeth chattered in his head as he
seized me by the chin.

'O! Don't cut my throat, sir,' I pleaded in terror. 'Pray don't do
it, sir.'

'Tell us your name!' said the man. 'Quick!' 50

'Pip, sir.'

'Once more,' said the man, staring at me. 'Give it mouth!'

'Pip. Pip, sir.'

'Show us where you live,' said the man. 'Pint out the place!'

I pointed to where our village lay, on the flat in-shore among 55
the alder-trees and pollards, a mile or more from the church.

The man, after looking at me for a moment, turned me upside
down and emptied my pockets. There was nothing in them but a

piece of bread. When the church came to itself—for he was so
sudden and strong that he made it go head over heels before me, 60
and I saw the steeple under my feet—when the church came to
itself, I say, I was seated on a high tombstone, trembling, while he
ate the bread ravenously.

'You young dog,' said the man, licking his lips, 'what fat cheeks
you ha' got.' 65

I believe they were fat, though I was at that time undersized, for
my years, and not strong.

'Darn Me if I couldn't eat 'em,' said the man, with a threatening
shake of his head, 'and if I han't half a mind to't!'

I earnestly expressed my hope that he wouldn't, and held 70
tighter to the tombstone on which he had put me; partly, to keep
myself upon it; partly, to keep myself from crying.

Charles Dickens: *Great Expectations*

2 This is the first sample of prose used in this unit. The two features of the text we
would like to focus on are:
a) setting;
b) verbal exchange/dialogue.
Work in groups. Select all features of the text which you may wish to
incorporate into the setting (which will be filmed on location). Begin with:
a) 'the churchyard';
b) 'the marsh country';
c) 'a . . . raw afternoon towards evening'.
When the above is complete, proceed to the dialogue. For this work in pairs,
then finalise in the same groups as for the 'setting' above. Begin:

> Man: Hold your noise! Keep still you little devil, or I'll cut your
> throat!
> Pip: O! Don't cut my throat, sir!

Note that not all of the verbal interchange is necessarily given in direct speech in
the text. You may be able to add other lines to the dialogue. Thus:

> Man: Show us where you live. Pint out the place!

> 'I pointed to where our village lay.'

This could be part of the dialogue with, for example, a line such as:

> Pip: O . . . o . . . ver there, sir!

3 Now decide on the pauses between each line in the dialogue. Remember the
impact of pauses, and look back if necessary at *Last to Go* by Pinter
(*Scenario III*).

≫→

4 Still working in groups, decide on how each of the lines is to be spoken. Which
   are loud, which are soft etc.?
   Choose two readers from each group and let them practise reading the dialogue
   for your scenario. The remainder of the group should suggest improvements.
   Further practice for reading aloud is given in Unit 4.

5 Return to the setting. Pip is introduced by Dickens in reported form, as in a
   biography:
   > 'I called myself Pip.'

   Consider if it is necessary to do this for the film. If so you must make Pip the
      speaker, and prepare his spoken part.
   How long/short should it be?
   Consider camera movements and lighting.
   Consider (from the text, not from the picture) the clothes worn by the 'stranger'
      and by Pip.

6 Decide on the time to be allowed for:
   a) the opening, before the 'stranger's' appearance;
   b) the whole scene.

7 Here is the remainder of the chapter. Read it at least twice.

> 'Now lookee here!' said the man. 'Where's your mother?'
>
> 'There, sir!' said I.
>
> He started, made a short run, and stopped and looked over his
> shoulder.
>
> 'There, sir!' I timidly explained. 'Also Georgiana. That's my   5
> mother.'
>
> 'Oh!' said he, coming back. 'And is that your father alonger
> your mother?'
>
> 'Yes, sir,' said I; 'him too; late of this parish.'
>
> 'Ha!' he muttered then, considering. 'Who d'ye live with—   10
> supposin' you're kindly let to live, which I han't made up my mind
> about?'
>
> 'My sister, sir—Mrs. Joe Gargery—wife of Joe Gargery, the
> blacksmith, sir.'
>
> 'Blacksmith, eh?' said he. And looked down at his leg.   15
>
> After darkly looking at his leg and at me several times, he came
> closer to my tombstone, took me by both arms, and tilted me back
> as far as he could hold me; so that his eyes looked most powerfully
> down into mine, and mine looked most helplessly up into his.
>
> 'Now lookee here,' he said, 'the question being whether you're   20
> to be let to live. You know what a file is?'
>
> 'Yes, sir.'
>
> 'And you know what wittles is?'
>
> 'Yes, sir.'

After each question he tilted me over a little more, so as to give   25
me a greater sense of helplessness and danger.

'You get me a file.' He tilted me again. 'And you get me wittles.'
He tilted me again. 'You bring 'em both to me.' He tilted me
again. 'Or I'll have your heart and liver out.' He tilted me again.

I was dreadfully frightened, and so giddy that I clung to him   30
with both hands, and said, 'If you would kindly please to let me
keep upright, sir, perhaps I shouldn't be sick, and perhaps I could
attend more.'

He gave me a most tremendous dip and roll, so that the church
jumped over its own weather-cock. Then, he held me by the arms   35
in an upright position on the top of the stone, and went on in these
fearful terms:

'You bring me, to-morrow morning early, that file and them
wittles. You bring the lot to me, at that old Battery over yonder.
You do it, and you never dare to say a word or dare to make a sign   40
concerning your having seen such a person as me, or any person
sumever, and you shall be let to live. You fail, or you go from my
words and in any partickler, no matter how small it is, and your
heart and your liver shall be tore out, roasted and ate. Now, I ain't
alone, as you may think I am. There's a young man hid with me, in   45
comparison with which young man I am a Angel. That young man
hears the words I speak. That young man has a secret way
pecooliar to himself, of getting at a boy, and at his heart, and at his
liver. It is in wain for a boy to attempt to hide himself from that
young man. A boy may lock his door, may be warm in bed, may   50
tuck himself up, may draw the clothes over his head, may think
himself comfortable and safe, but that young man will softly creep
and creep his way to him and tear him open. I am a keeping that
young man from harming of you at the present moment, with great
difficulty. I find it wery hard to hold that young man off of your   55
inside. Now, what do you say?'

I said that I would get him the file, and I would get him what
broken bits of food I could, and I would come to him at the
Battery, early in the morning.

'Say, Lord strike you dead if you don't!' said the man.   60

I said so, and he took me down.

'Now,' he pursued, 'you remember what you've undertook, and
you remember that young man, and you get home!'

'Goo-good night sir,' I faltered.

'Much of that!' said he, glancing about him over the cold wet   65
flat. 'I wish I was a frog. Or a eel!'

At the same time, he hugged his shuddering body in both his
arms—clasping himself, as if to hold himself together—and
limped towards the low church wall. As I saw him go, picking his
way among the nettles, and among the brambles that bound the   70

green mounds, he looked in my young eyes as if he were eluding the hands of the dead people, stretching up cautiously out of the their graves, to get a twist upon his ankle and pull him in.

When he came to the low church wall, he got over it, like a man whose legs were numbed and stiff, and then turned round to look 75 for me. When I saw him turning, I set my face towards home, and made the best use of my legs. But presently I looked over my shoulder, and saw him going on again towards the river, still hugging himself in both arms, and picking his way with his sore feet among the great stones dropped into the marshes here and 80 there, for stepping-places when the rains were heavy, or the tide was in.

The marshes were just a long black horizontal line then, as I stopped to look after him; and the river was just another horizontal line, not nearly so broad nor yet so black; and the sky was just a row 85 of long angry red lines and dense black lines intermixed. On the edge of the river I could faintly make out the only two black things in all the prospect that seemed to be standing upright; one of these was the beacon by which the sailors steered—like an unhooped cask upon a pole—an ugly thing when you were near it; the other a 90 gibbet, with some chains hanging to it which had once held a pirate. The man was limping on towards this latter, as if he were the pirate come to life, and come down, and going back to hook himself up again. It gave me a terrible turn when I thought so; and as I saw the cattle lifting their heads to gaze after him, I wondered 95 whether they thought so too. I looked all round for the horrible young man, and could see no signs of him. But now I was frightened again, and ran home without stopping.

Charles Dickens: *Great Expectations*

8 Work in groups. List briefly the features which will be *un*changed:
a) characters;
b) clothing;
  etc.
Then apply these points (see 2–7 above):
a) dialogue;
b) pauses;
c) how each response should be spoken;
d) time;
e) action(s) which are not linguistic, for example:
    '. . . he hugged his shuddering body in both his arms – clasping himself, as
    if to hold himself together – and limped towards the low church wall.'
Mark all actions or movements of this kind.
f) editing;
g) conclusion: decide on the final pictures of the first scene (which will also be
   the end of the first chapter).

EXPLOITATION

1 Review the whole of your scenario after a few days and a single re-reading of Chapter 1 of *Great Expectations* and see if you can think of any improvements, or ways of increasing 'impact'.

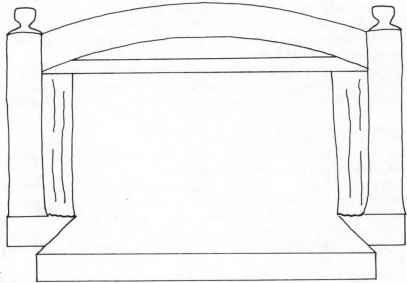

Figure I

2 Finally, we return to the question of movement on stage and this time to the physical position of characters in a drama in relation to each other, the audience, and the open space of the stage itself. First, make an enlarged version of the sketch in Figure I on a large sheet of paper.

Then reproduce the sketch in Figure II which divides up stage positions and gives them their usual abbreviations.

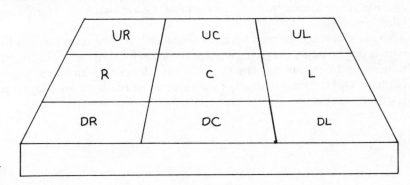

Figure II

Note: R – Right   C – Centre   L – Left   U – Upstage
D – Downstage is nearest the audience. Directions are therefore given from the actor's point of view.

3 Now return to the scene from *Macbeth* (*Scenario II*). Work in groups to decide how you would 'direct' the physical position of the two actors. For example:
Would they be close together?
Would they both be downstage or upstage?
Would they be left or right?
Would one of them be in the centre of the stage?
Would the centre of the stage be occupied for the whole scene?
How much movement about the stage would you want from *one* of the two characters or *both* of them?
Develop further questions for yourselves but base your decisions on close reference back to the text itself and on your interpretation of the characters' behaviour. Repeat the exercise with reference to *Last to Go* (*Scenario III*).

SUMMARY OF THE UNIT

1 We hope you have enjoyed your role as producer and director and have understood something of the skills involved.
2 To 'translate' a text into another medium it is important to read the text carefully. Your 'pictures' of it depend on responses to and interpretation of the whole text, but you are influenced by individual words too.
3 You should have experienced directly some of the differences between text, film and theatre as media for the transmission of messages, and also have recognised how they can be related.
4 Some of the texts and authors used for this approach are examined again in other units. For example, 'Meeting at Night' is examined for its grammatical patterns in Unit 5 (*Language patterns II*). 'Ozymandias' is the subject for a ranking exercise in Unit 3 (*Orientation*); another extract from *Macbeth* is examined for its 'performance' in Unit 4 (*Reading aloud III*); Pinter's *Last to Go* is a very interesting text to try to summarise (Unit 1) and might be compared in this respect with 'Cat in the Rain' in Unit 1 (*Summary I*). You may like to produce a 'scenario' for the extract from Shakespeare's *Othello* used in Unit 10 (*Forum II*) or for the 'picture' of Dickens' Coketown from *Hard Times* Unit 3, (*Ranking III*).
5 There is more to reading a text, and *especially a play*, than just reading the words on the page. Plays are written to be performed and gain an extra and vital dimension from staging. The visual can reinforce and further symbolise the content, and the imagination of the director or reader is an integral part of the creative process.

Unit 3   Talking together: Ranking

Introduction for the student

The aim of this unit is to encourage you to talk more about literary texts. Most of
the exercises involve you in an activity we call 'ranking'. This is a way of getting
you to list your impressions, ideas and feelings about a text in an order of
importance or impact. It also means that you must defend your ranking against
those of other readers (usually in your group) who may decide on a different order.
Most of the activities lead directly into oral discussion.

Orientation

1   The first text is the well-known poem 'Ozymandias' by Shelley (see Unit 2).
Imagine that you meet a group of people who have travelled to many parts of the
world, not just to places which can be reached easily by international airlines,
but to places which are still far from airports, roads, railways or other facilities.
These people like to talk of their travels and their experiences. One image
particularly which sticks in their minds is of a once enormous statue, now in
ruins. Where in the world might it be possible to find a statue like this? In this
case it is only the ruins of the statue which have survived. Whatever else was
there previously has long since disappeared. The traveller is particularly
impressed by the size of the statue. Here are some words which indicate how big
the statue was:
   a big statue
   a massive statue
   a vast statue
   a colossal statue
   a large statue
   a huge statue
Only two of these adjectives actually occur in the poem. In the above list put (1)
beside the phrase which to you gives the greatest impression of size. Then choose
what seems to be the second and third largest, marking them (2) and (3). (This is
the process we call ranking and is the basis of this unit.)

2 Here is the poem:

 *

> I MET a traveller from an antique land
> Who said: Two vast and trunkless legs of stone
> Stand in the desert . . . Near them, on the sand,
> Half sunk, a shattered visage lies, whose frown,
> And wrinkled lip, and sneer of cold command,   5
> Tell that its sculptor well those passions read
> Which yet survive, stamped on these lifeless things,
> The hand that mocked them, and the heart that fed:
> And on the pedestal these words appear:
> 'My name is Ozymandias, king of kings: 10
> Look on my works, ye Mighty, and despair!'
> Nothing beside remains. Round the decay
> Of that colossal wreck, boundless and bare
> The lone and level sands stretch far away.

> Percy Bysshe Shelley

Note that 'antique' in line 1 corresponds to 'ancient' in contemporary English.
   How does the poet convey the great size of the statue other than by the use of the two adjectives 'vast' and 'colossal'?

3 The traveller is impressed above all else by the expression on the face of the statue, which seems to indicate what kind of man Ozymandias was.
What kind of man do you think Ozymandias was?
Complete the following table, indicating which statements are true, which false, or, if you are not certain, tick the column headed (?).

	T	F	(?)
a) O. was a kind and benevolent king.			
b) O. was a cruel king.			
c) O. was an unhappy king.			
d) O. was a king who killed lots of people.			
e) O. was a king who expected people to do what he said.			
f) O. liked sculpture. He appreciated its beauty.			
g) O. was a passionate king.			
h) O. was an immortal.			

Discuss your answers with another student. Reach agreement on how the table should be completed.

* The recording is to be found within Unit 2.

4 In the 'true–false' exercise on 'Ozymandias' above it would also be possible to put the statements in order of importance, according to your reading of the poem; in other words, to rank them. Before applying this procedure to literary text, however, try it first as a language exercise.

ORAL WORK: Ranking

A group of important visitors are coming to visit your country. You want them to gain some understanding of your culture and also have a good impression of your country. Choose six places you will take them to and then rank the places in order of importance (not in the order   5 of seeing them). First work individually, then in small groups. Each group must produce its ranked list of six places which all members of that group agree on. Then the class works together as a whole. Each group reports and the whole class tries to agree on one list.   10

Long & Nation: *Readthru'*

In this exercise the ranking you finally agreed on was presumably the result of the most persuasive argument. When you apply the same procedure to literary text, one person's argument may be very convincing, but you must all have read the text extremely closely to be able to form your own judgement and to justify it.

Ranking I

1 As the title of the following poem indicates, it is about a village schoolmaster. It was written in the eighteenth century in rhymed couplets. Begin by picking out some of the information given about this man. Do not be discouraged by the apparent difficulty of lines 1 and 2. Begin with line 4:
   'The village master . . .'
a) Did what?
b) Where?
c) What ability did he have?
d) Where was the building mentioned in (b)?

2 Listen to the poem and try to form an image of the schoolmaster.

3 Read the poem carefully. If it helps you, rephrase the sentences within the poem in modern English, and with, as far as possible, normal word order.

The Village Schoolmaster

Beside yon straggling fence that skirts the way,
With blossomed furze unprofitably gay,
There, in his noisy mansion, skill'd to rule,
The village master taught his little school;
A man severe he was, and stern to view,   5
I knew him well, and every truant knew;
Well had the boding tremblers learned to trace
The day's disasters in his morning face;
Full well they laugh'd with counterfeited glee,
At all his jokes, for many a joke had he;   10
Full well the busy whisper circling round,
Conveyed the dismal tidings when he frowned:
Yet he was kind, or if severe in aught,
The love he bore to learning was in fault;
The village all declared how much he knew;   15
'Twas certain he could write, and cipher too;
Lands he could measure, terms and tides presage,
And e'en the story ran that he could gauge.
In arguing too, the parson owned his skill,
For e'en tho' vanquished, he could argue still;   20
While words of learned length, and thundering sound,
Amazed the gazing rustics ranged around,
And still they gazed, and still the wonder grew,
That one small head could carry all he knew.

Oliver Goldsmith

4 Most of us have a stereotyped image of a schoolteacher, probably influenced by someone from our own childhood. To what extent does this schoolmaster correspond with the image you yourself have of a schoolteacher? (How is he like your image? How is he different?)

5 Rank the following statements in order of importance to indicate what you think are the most significant characteristics of the schoolmaster in the poem. Rank only six statements. Leave out the remainder. If you think there is an important point which is not listed below, you may add it.
a) The schoolmaster was strict.
b) Everybody was afraid of him.
c) He was frequently in a bad temper.
d) He was jolly and amusing.
e) He made jokes all the time.
f) He was friendly, but could be angry at times.

g) He was kind.
h) He was very dedicated.
i) Above everything he wanted his students to learn well.
j) Everyone in the village admired him.
k) He had a good grasp of many subjects, especially at junior level.
l) He liked to discuss important matters with other people.
m) He used many big words.
n) Pupils liked to listen to him.
o) He was wasted in such a small and remote place.

6 Compare and discuss in groups. Speak English where possible.

7 Reach consensus.

8 Reconvene as a single group. Again reach consensus.

EXPLOITATION

1 Consider to what extent you think the schoolmaster is like a modern
  schoolteacher in an English speaking country (Britain, United States, Australia
  etc.) in :
  a) a rural community;
  b) a big city school.

2 Compare the schoolmaster with a similar figure in your own culture/society in
  the present day. What are the similarities, if any?

Ranking II

The next poem in this unit is 'An Irish Airman Foresees his Death' by W. B. Yeats.
This poem might also have a place in Unit 9, where some background information
is almost a necessity for an understanding of the text. However, a few points only
will be given here:
a) It is a war poem, and refers to the First World War (see Unit 9, *Background*). It
   is worth noting that aeroplanes were as yet little developed in 1914, and were
   dangerous and unreliable.
b) One key to the poem is in the title 'An *Irish* Airman'. Ireland was not directly
   involved in the War, and the feelings of patriotism did not therefore touch the
   narrator, the 'I' of the poem. 'Kiltartan Cross', and 'Kiltartan's poor' are
   references to a place in Ireland.
c) W. B. Yeats (1865–1939) was himself Irish.

1 Listen to the poem, then read it through several times. Query with your teacher
  any lines which seem obscure.

An Irish Airman Foresees his Death

I know that I shall meet my fate
Somewhere among the clouds above;
Those that I fight I do not hate,
Those that I guard I do not love;
My country is Kiltartan Cross,   5
My countrymen Kiltartan's poor,
No likely end could bring them loss
Or leave them happier than before.
Nor law, nor duty bade me fight,
Nor public men, nor cheering crowds,   10
A lonely impulse of delight
Drove to this tumult in the clouds;
I balanced all, brought all to mind,
The years to come seemed waste of breath,
A waste of breath the years behind   15
In balance with this life, this death.

W. B. Yeats

2 Now look at this list of statements and, first, mark those which correlate with lines in the poem and those which do not.
a) He felt indifferent to the enemy.
b) He did not fight for the sake of national security.
c) He was prepared to fight for the honour of Ireland.
d) He saw no glamour in war.
e) He was attracted by the excitement of flying.
f) He was a great 'loner'.
g) He was dissatisfied with his life before the war.
h) He was opposed to the waste of war.
i) Death in action seemed preferable to death by other means.
j) He lacked a sense of balance, or proportion, about life and death.

The above statements are more mixed than the corresponding items on 'The Village Schoolmaster' (*Ranking I* above). In the latter it is possible to rank the items which we consider most important in any schoolteacher, but in this example we are looking more at our underlying impressions of (a) the poet (What makes him tell us this?) and (b) the airman (What made him volunteer for war?).

Work in pairs. Rank the three statements which best illustrate the confused and tortured state of mind of the 'airman'. Select the point which makes the strongest or most powerful impression on you when you hear or read the poem.

3 Now work in groups of six or eight. Reach consensus on the rank order of items 1–3.

Ranking III

1 This prose example is taken from the opening of Chapter 5 of *Hard Times* by
  Charles Dickens. It describes 'Coketown', the fictitious town in which the main
  action of the novel takes place. Use the picture to help you build an impression
  of an English industrial town in the nineteenth century.

Though all the features of the town are mentioned – building material, canal and
river, factories, churches, streets, town hall, jail, and people, – it is not an
'ordinary' description. Though there are frequent references to fact, the
description contains relatively few facts, the exception being one sentence of
detail about the New Church – largely because that building was different from
the rest of the town. The description consists of a series of impressions (as with
the descriptions of the many characters in Dickens' novels). From these
impressions the reader is unconsciously invited to perform his or her own
ranking exercise, and to decide which impression overrides the others.

 First read the extract carefully. Do not stop for any words, sentences, or
references which you do not understand.

> COKETOWN, to which Messrs Bounderby and Gradgrind now
> walked, was a triumph of fact; it had no greater taint of fancy in it
> than Mrs Gradgrind herself. Let us strike the key-note, Coke-
> town, before pursuing our tune.
> It was a town of red brick, or of brick that would have been red if   5
> the smoke and ashes had allowed it; but, as matters stood it was a
> town of unnatural red and black like the painted face of a savage. It
> was a town of machinery and tall chimneys, out of which
> interminable serpents of smoke trailed themselves for ever and

ever, and never got uncoiled. It had a black canal in it, and a river   10
that ran purple with ill-smelling dye, and vast piles of building full
of windows where there was a rattling and a trembling all day long,
and where the piston of the steam-engine worked monotonously
up and down, like the head of an elephant in a state of melancholy
madness. It contained several large streets all very like one   15
another, and many small streets still more like one another,
inhabited by people equally like one another, who all went in and
out at the same hours, with the same sound upon the same
pavements, to do the same work, and to whom every day was the
same as yesterday and tomorrow, and every year the counterpart of   20
the last and the next.

These attributes of Coketown were in the main inseparable
from the work by which it was sustained; against them were to be
set off, comforts of life which found their way all over the world,
and elegancies of life which made, we will not ask how much of the   25
fine lady, who could scarcely bear to hear the place mentioned.
The rest of its features were voluntary, and they were these.

You saw nothing in Coketown but what was severely workful. If
the members of a religious persuasion built a chapel there—as the
members of eighteen religious persuasions had done—they made it   30
a pious warehouse of red brick, with sometimes (but this only in
highly ornamented examples) a bell in a bird-cage on the top of it.
The solitary exception was the New Church; a stuccoed edifice
with a square steeple over the door, terminating in four short
pinnacles like florid wooden legs. All the public inscriptions in the   35
town were painted alike, in severe characters of black and white.
The jail might have been the infirmary, the infirmary might have
been the jail, the town-hall might have been either, or both, or
anything else, for anything that appeared to the contrary in the
graces of their construction. Fact, fact, fact, everywhere in the   40
material aspect of the town; fact, fact, fact, everywhere in the
immaterial. The M'Choakumchild school was all fact, and the
school of design was all fact, and the relations between master and
man were all fact, and everything was fact between the lying-in
hospital and the cemetery, and what you couldn't state in figures,   45
or show to be purchaseable in the cheapest market and saleable in
the dearest, was not, and never should be, world without end,
Amen.

Charles Dickens: *Hard Times*

2 Read the instructions very carefully before you begin the task.

A list of impressions of Coketown follows. Some of these correspond with the
text and some do not (i.e. some are 'true' and some are 'false'). Check each

against the text itself, and cross out those which do *not* reflect the impressions portrayed by Dickens. Work individually.

a) Coketown was a colourful place.
b) Coketown was a drab place.
c) Coketown was dull and monotonous.
d) Coketown was lively and dynamic.
e) Coketown was a depressing place.
f) Coketown was a place of great comfort and affluence.
g) The buildings of Coketown were varied, with many religious buildings.
h) The buildings of Coketown were all similar, and mostly lacked distinction.
i) The people of Coketown did not welcome strangers.
j) The people of Coketown were religious.
k) The people of Coketown were of low moral standards.
l) The people of Coketown were totally irreligious.
m) The people of Coketown demanded the best of everything.

3 Compare with another student and see if you agree on your final list of 'impressions'.
Still working with your partner rank the three most important impressions in the list.

4 Combine the three rank items into a single sentence. Do not worry about their order, but try and produce a well-constructed English sentence. This, in practice, should produce a summary of the text.

5 Join with another pair and compare sentences. Justify your choice and then, together, work out the best possible sentence. Your teacher will write each group's sentence on the board. As a class, you must reach consensus on which sentence gives the best impression of Coketown, while still following the Dickens original.

EXPLOITATION

1 Read Chapters 1–5 of *Hard Times*.
Who are Mr Bounderby and Mr Gradgrind?
Write a short description, of about paragraph length, of each.

2 Make notes on the similarities and the differences between the picture on page 47 and Dickens' description of Coketown. If you photographed a town or painted a picture based on Dickens' Coketown, how would you do it and why would you do it like that?

Ranking IV

1 In this section we return briefly to poetry, with D. H. Lawrence's poem 'Snake', though the poem is loosely structured and has some of the features of prose.

As an introductory step (not connected directly with the ranking exercise which follows) consider which lines are, or could be, prose, and which have marked poetic qualities. As a starting point consider the two lines:

He reached down from a fissure in the earth-wall in the gloom.
And trailed his yellow-brown slackness soft-bellied down.

Which line is 'prose' and which poetry? What features make it poetic? (Word order, word choice, word formation, 'sound' (see Unit 4), other features?)

The poem presents few difficulties of 'interpretation'. The poet/author watches a snake come to drink and examines his feelings towards the creature and presents us with an interesting range of impressions.

In *Ranking III* we were concerned with Dickens' impressions of Coketown. Here we are more concerned with your personal, individual impressions of a poem.

Before you read the poem look at the picture of the snake on page 117. Discuss the picture with another student. Make notes on what you both like and dislike about snakes.

2 Lines 1–15 of the poem are printed beneath. Read these carefully.

Snake

A snake came to my water-trough
On a hot, hot day, and I in pyjamas for the heat,
To drink there.

In the deep, strange-scented shade of the great dark
   carob-tree
I came down the steps with my pitcher   5
And must wait, must stand and wait, for there he was at the
   trough before me.

He reached down from a fissure in the earth-wall in the gloom
And trailed his yellow-brown slackness soft-bellied down,
   over the edge of the stone trough
And rested his throat upon the stone bottom,
And where the water had dripped from the tap, in a small   10
   clearness,
He sipped with his straight mouth,
Softly drank through his straight gums, into his slack long
   body,
Silently.

Someone was before me at my water-trough,
And I, like a second comer, waiting.   15

So the snake has come to drink at the water trough, and the poet describes this.
As you read this the impression you get of the scene is:
a) the heat;
b) the beauty, both of the rural setting and of the snake;
c) fear – what is going to happen?
d) movement, as the snake 'trailed his yellow-brown slackness . . . down';
e) gracefulness;
f) loneliness and silence;
g) frustration at not being able to get to the water, and having to wait;
h) indignation – the snake is an interloper.

Now rank the three most powerful of these. Find words in the poem to support
your first choice. You may add another impression if you think there is one not
listed, but you should be able to find words in the poem to justify it.

3 Here are the next 19 lines of the poem. Read them as before.

> He lifted his head from his drinking, as cattle do,
> And looked at me vaguely, as drinking cattle do,
> And flickered his two-forked tongue from his lips, and mused
>   a moment,
> And stooped and drank a little more,
> Being earth-brown, earth-golden from the burning, burning   20
>   bowels of the earth,
> On the day of Sicilian July, with Etna smoking.
>
> The voice of my education said to me
> He must be killed,
> For in Sicily the black, black snakes are innocent, the gold are
>   venomous.
>
> And voices in me said, If you were a man   25
> You would take a stick and break him now, and finish him off.
> But must I confess how I liked him,
> How glad I was he had come like a guest in quiet, to drink at
>   my water-trough
> And depart peaceful, pacified, and thankless,
> Into the burning bowels of this earth?   30
>
> Was it cowardice, that I dared not kill him?
> Was it perversity, that I longed to talk to him?
> Was it humility, to feel so honoured?
> I felt so honoured.

Follow the same procedure as in number 2.
First, give a brief one-sentence summary of these lines. Then consider this list of
impressions (you may add others if you wish) of the whole of this section.

⟫→

51

Choose the three you find most powerful and rank them:
a) the closeness of the snake;
b) fear of the snake;
c) self-defence;
d) reacting to the snake;
e) secret love;
f) cowardice;
g) confusion – mixed feelings in this unusual situation.

4 The remainder of the poem follows. Read on.

> And yet those voices: 35
> *'If you were not afraid, you would kill him!'*
>
> And truly I was afraid, I was most afraid,
> But even so, honoured still more
> That he should seek my hospitality
> From out of the dark door of the secret earth. 40
>
> He drank enough
> And lifted his head, dreamily, as one who has drunken,
> And flicked his tongue like a forked night on the air, so
>   black,
> Seeming to lick his lips,
> And looked around like a god, unseeing, into the air, 45
> And slowly turned his head,
> And slowly, very slowly, as if thrice adream,
> Proceeded to draw his slow length curving round
> And climb again the broken bank of my wall-face.
>
> And as he put his head into that dreadful hole, 50
> And as he slowly drew up, snake-easing his shoulders, and
>   entered farther,
> A sort of horror, a sort of protest against his withdrawing into
>   that horrid black hole,
> Deliberately going into the blackness, and slowly drawing
>   himself after,
> Overcame me now his back was turned.
>
> I looked round, I put down my pitcher, 55
> I picked up a clumsy log
> And threw it at the water-trough with a clatter.
>
> I think it did not hit him,
> But suddenly that part of him that was left behind convulsed
>   in undignified haste,
> Writhed like lightning, and was gone 60
> Into that black hole, the earth-lipped fissure in the wall-front,
> At which, in the intense still noon, I stared with fascination.

And immediately I regretted it.
I thought how paltry, how vulgar, what a mean act!
I despised myself and the voices of my accursed human   65
      education.

And I thought of the albatross,
And I wished he would come back, my snake.

For he seemed to me again like a king,
Like a king in exile, uncrowned in the underworld,
Now due to be crowned again.   70

And so, I missed my chance with one of the lords
Of life.
And I have something to expiate;
A pettiness.

D. H. Lawrence

A suggested summary is:
   The snake finished drinking, and as it was going into a hole the narrator threw
   a stick at it, but then regretted his action, as the snake had done him no harm.

5 Work in groups. List eight of your impressions of this part of the poem. Do not
   try and rank them until the group agrees on the list. Use phrases to expand your
   impressions if necessary (e.g. the beauty, both of the rural setting and of the
   snake).

6 Working individually, rank your three strongest impressions from the list. Then
   pair with a reader from another group, and compare your rank items for this
   section (the final part of the poem). See to what extent your impressions and
   ranking correspond.

EXPLOITATION

Nine lines from the end of the poem you find the line:
         'And I thought of the albatross'
Why *the* albatross (not *an* albatross)?
What is the literary reference here?
What is the connection between the *snake* of this poem, and the *albatross*?

SUMMARY OF THE UNIT

Briefly, the aims of this unit have been to:
a) encourage more confident and fluent discussion about literary texts;
b) provide a basis for discussion through the use of lists of statements to be
    ranked;
c) show that careful reference to the text is needed to support arguments and that
    mere impressions and feelings on their own are not enough.

Unit 4   Read it aloud: Text and phonology

Introduction for the student

This unit is designed to help you explore some of the factors involved in reading a literary text aloud. Just as writers exploit grammar and vocabulary for literary effect, so they pattern sounds for expressive purposes. This is a feature which can best be brought out by reading aloud, and many literary texts gain from this element of 'performance'.

You will find the cassette particularly useful for this unit.

Orientation

There are many different ways of reading a text. Factors such as speed, pitch and emotion all help to convey the reader's interpretation of the piece. Below is a set of eight such 'variables' (you may think of more) which the reader can select from and combine to give added meaning to the words on the page.

i)   loud   — soft
ii)   fast   — slow
iii) high pitch — low pitch
iv)   tense   — relaxed
v)   smiling   — grim
vi)   'chin up'   — 'chin down'
vii) emotive   — non-emotive
viii) 'breathy'

The first five pairs above are probably self-explanatory. The following brief notes are added for the remainder:

vi)   Consider the exchange:
      A: My father died last night.
      B: I'm sorry to hear that.

Utterance B here is likely to be spoken with 'chin down'. It is also likely to be soft rather than loud. For 'chin-up' consider:
      'I am proud to announce that your company has again achieved . . .'

vii) If I say, 'Take the second turning to the left' that is likely to be non-emotive, and as such 'neutral'. 'Emotive' would include any utterance which involved the expression of emotions such as excitement, anger, disappointment etc.

viii) 'Breathy' refers to the mode of speaking frequently associated with television advertising and intended to be persuasive and, in some cases, sexy. There is no obvious 'opposite' to 'breathy' to form a pair.

Reading aloud I

1 Listen to this reading of 'The General' by Siegfried Sassoon. We shall look at this poem again in Unit 6 where we examine associations of particular words. Here we concentrate on how to express the meaning orally.
   Now look at the poem and read it through chorally.

The General

'Good-morning; good-morning!' the General said
When we met him last week on our way to the line.
Now the soldiers he smiled at are most of 'em dead,
And we're cursing his staff for incompetent swine.
'He's a cheery old card,' grunted Harry to Jack   5
As they slogged up to Arras with rifle and pack.

★

But he did for them both by his plan of attack.

Siegfried Sassoon

2 Consider the following features and practise them in groups. Make comments on each other's performance.
   Line 1 Greeting high pitch, 'The General said' low pitch.
   Greeting also 'chin up'. Try and speak as a superior speaking to inferiors or subordinates.
   Line 2 Continue low pitch, quick rather than slow. No variation of pitch.
   Consider also loud versus soft, tense versus slack.
   Line 3 Grim. Stress on 'dead'. Very tense; relaxed speaking loses the meaning entirely.
   Line 4 Grimmer than 3. Definitely emotive (anger? contempt?). Consider especially the articulation* of the word 'swine' (and also its associations – see Unit 6, Section A, *Orientation*).
   Line 5 Complete change from 4. First part of line smiling – 'chin up' – in spite of the verb 'grunted'. Remainder of line low pitch.
   Line 6 Less marked than any other line, but consider loud versus soft, quick versus slow.
   For effect, follow by a pause of a full three seconds, and time this.
   Line 7 Tense, but lacking the bitterness of 4. Soft – appropriate to the presence of death.

* articulation – the way the word is spoken.

3 Now listen again to the recorded reading of the poem. See if you agree or disagree with the features listed above. Are different readings possible while still expressing 'the sense' of the poem?

Reading aloud II

1 The poem in this section is called 'Song of the River', by Charles Kingsley. Though skilfully constructed it is included not so much for its literary value as for the contrasts suggested in the articulation. Consider, first, a summary of each stanza, and which of the variables of articulation are implied. Work in groups.

Stanza 1

The river flows through the countryside, far from the town. The water is clear and fresh, flowing quickly in shallow places, slowly in the deeper parts.

quick versus slow?
tense versus slack?
loud versus soft?
any emotive features?

Stanza 2

The river is badly polluted as it flows through a smoky town. The water and the surroundings are dirty. The sparkle of its early progress is completely lost.

Which of the above variables are most likely to apply when the poem is read aloud? What changes from stanza 1?

Stanza 3

The river breaks free of the city and moves on more quickly towards the sea. The sea has a cleansing effect and the river gets a new vitality, but different from the early stages, in stanza 1.

As above, stanza 2.

2 Remain in your groups. Listen to the recording of the poem. Here is the text:

    CLEAR and cool, clear and cool,
        By laughing shallow, and dreaming pool;
    Cool and clear, cool and clear,
      By shining shingle, and foaming weir;
  Under the crag where the ouzel sings,   5
  And the ivied wall where the church-bell rings,
      Undefiled, for the undefiled;
    Play by me, bathe in me, mother and child.

      Dank and foul, dank and foul,
    By the smoky town in its murky cowl;   10
      Foul and dank, foul and dank,
    By wharf and sewer and slimy bank;

Darker and darker the further I go,
Baser and baser the richer I grow;
 Who dare sport with the sin-defiled?   15
Shrink from me, turn from me, mother and child.

 Strong and free, strong and free;
The flood-gates are open, away to the sea.
 Free and strong, free and strong,
 Cleansing my streams as I hurry along   20
To the golden sands, and the leaping bar,
And the taintless tide that awaits me afar,
Till I lose myself in the infinite main,
Like a soul that has sinned and is pardoned again.
 Undefiled, for the undefiled;   25
Play by me, bathe in me, mother and child.

Charles Kingsley

Read the poem chorally, each group in turn reading one stanza, the others listening.

Listen again to the recorded reading.

3 Now, working individually, note on the text any features which are particularly distinctive. For example:
   'Clear and cool, clear and cool' ‖ *very slow*
                 soft
                 low pitch

There is no need to comment on every line as in *Reading aloud I*. Look only for prominent features. Discuss in groups the features you have marked.

Reading aloud III

1 This extract is from Shakespeare's play *Macbeth*. The situation is as follows: Macbeth attends a banquet. Just before this he has arranged – successfully – the murder of Banquo, whom he thought a rival. The lords at the banquet invite Macbeth to sit down, and indicate where he should sit. But sitting in the place which they indicate, Macbeth, and no one else, sees the ghost of Banquo!
Here is the text:

MACBETH   Sweet remembrancer!
 Now good digestion wait on appetite,
 And health on both!
 LENNOX   May't please your highness sit.
  Enter the Ghost of Banquo and sits in
  Macbeth's place

MACBETH

Here had we now our country's honour roofed,
Were the graced person of our Banquo present;   5
Who may I rather challenge for unkindness
Than pity for mischance.

ROSS   His absence, sir,
Lays blame upon his promise. Please't your highness
To grace us with your royal company?

MACBETH

The table's full.   10

LENNOX   Here is a place reserved, sir.

MACBETH

Where?

LENNOX

Here, my good lord. What is't that moves your highness?

MACBETH

Which of you have done this?

LORDS   What, my good lord?

MACBETH

Thou canst not say I did it; never shake
Thy gory locks at me.   15

ROSS

Gentlemen, rise. His highness is not well.

William Shakespeare: *Macbeth* (III, iv)

2 Consider the features of articulation for each part of this scene. Pay special attention to:
   a) 'Were the graced person of our Banquo present.'
      (Remember Macbeth knows that Banquo is dead.)
   b) 'Which of you have done this?'
      What is the language function of this line?
      It is certainly not 'asking for information'.
      What is the emotion expressed?
      What variables are likely to be involved?
   Make a recording of the scene and play it back. Comment on the performance of the speakers, saying whether an utterance is too loud, not loud enough etc. Comment particularly on the articulation of 'Which of you have done this?'

EXPLOITATION

If you do not know the play of *Macbeth* write down how you think Macbeth gets out of this disturbing situation. Then read *Macbeth* Act III Scene 4. Make a summary (see Unit 1 for guidance) of what in fact 'happens'.

Reading aloud IV

1 Here is the text of another war poem (see *Reading aloud I* above). The poem is from the same war, the First World War 1914–18. It incorporates many of the features of the literature of this war – bitterness, frustration, contempt for the high-ranking officer, anger, sadness at the loss of friends, feelings of futility (see also Unit 8, Section A, *Stylistic analysis* and Unit 9, *Background IV*). While these are implied in the 'words on the page', they can be brought out much more forcibly by the reader's expression of voice.
   Follow this procedure:
   a) Read the poem several times.
   b) Mark any lines where you think there are special sound patterns.
   c) Work in pairs: read alternate stanzas.
   d) Suggest changes or improvements to your partner's reading.
   e) Reverse roles, reading the part you did not read in (c); again suggest improvements.

      After the Battle

         So they are satisfied with our Brigade,
            And it remains to parcel out the bays!
         And we shall have the usual Thanks Parade,
            The beaming General, and the soapy praise.

         You will come up in your capricious car   5
            To find your heroes sulking in the rain,
         To tell us how magnificent we are,
            And how you hope we'll do the same again.

> And we, who knew your old abusive tongue,
>> Who heard you hector us a week before, 10
> We who have bled to boost you up a rung –
>> A K.C.B. perhaps, perhaps a Corps –
>
> We who must mourn those spaces in the mess,
>> And somehow fill those hollows in the heart,
> We do not want your Sermon on Success, 15
>> Your greasy benisons on Being Smart.
>
> We only want to take our wounds away.
>> To some warm village where the tumult ends,
> And drowsing in the sunshine many a day,
>> Forget our aches, forget that we had friends. 20
>
> Weary we are of blood and noise and pain;
>> This was a week we shall not soon forget;
> And if, indeed, we have to fight again,
>> We little wish to think about it yet.
>
> We have done well; we like to hear it said 25
>> Say it, and then, for God's sake, say no more.
> Fight, if you must, fresh battles far ahead,
>> But keep them dark behind your chateau door!
>
> A. P. Herbert

2 Now listen to the recorded reading of the poem 'After the Battle'.

3 Play it through again. Underline any words you hear as markedly 'grim' or
   'emotive'. Try and say what the emotion is. Check with your partner and see
   where you agree or disagree in your hearing of the poem.

Reading aloud V

1 The first example in this sub-section (i.e. prose read aloud for its sound patterns)
   is a famous passage from the story 'Youth' by Joseph Conrad. The situation is
   that a ship on its way to Bangkok catches fire and sinks in the Gulf of Thailand,
   after a journey in which a whole series of misfortunes has occurred. This section
   describes the sinking of the ship.

   The interesting feature is that Conrad tells the story through a narrator, so it
   is, theoretically, spoken language. Conrad's careful prose, however, is far
   removed from ordinary spoken narrative, though the richness of it can be further
   brought out by reading it aloud.

   First read it silently, and consider how you would read it. Imagine that later
   you are going to read it aloud on radio, and you want the words to be as
   descriptive as possible of the scene.

'But we did not make a start at once. We must see the last of the ship. And so the boats drifted about that night, heaving and setting on the swell. The men dozed, waked, sighed, groaned. I looked at the burning ship.

'Between the darkness of earth and heaven she was burning   5
fiercely upon a disc of purple sea shot by the blood-red play of gleams; upon a disc of water glittering and sinister. A high, clear flame, an immense and lonely flame, ascended from the ocean, and from its summit the black smoke poured continuously at the sky. She burned furiously; mournful and imposing like a funeral   10
pile kindled in the night, surrounded by the sea, watched over by the stars. A magnificent death had come like a grace, like a gift, like a reward to that old ship at the end of her laborious days. The surrender of her weary ghost to the keeping of stars and sea was stirring like the sight of a glorious triumph. The masts fell just   15
before daybreak, and for a moment there was a burst and turmoil of sparks that seemed to fill with flying fire the night patient and watchful, the vast night lying silent upon the sea . . .

'Then the oars were got out, and the boats forming in a line moved round her remains as if in procession – the long boat   20
leading. As we pulled across her stern a slim dart of fire shot out viciously at us, and suddenly she went down, head first, in a great hiss of steam. The unconsumed stern was the last to sink;

but the paint had gone, had cracked, had peeled off, and there
were no letters, there was no word, no stubborn device that was   25
like her soul, to flash at the rising sun her creed and her name.

Joseph Conrad: 'Youth'

2 Now listen to the recorded version of the text, and compare it with your own
intended articulation. Is it faster or slower, louder or softer, lower pitch or
higher pitch etc. than you anticipated? Examine the picture on page 61. Use your
response to the picture to help you decide.

3 There are many examples of lists, or alternatives, in the text:
       'A high, clear flame, an immense and lonely flame . . .'
       'A magnificent death had come like a grace, like a gift, like a reward . . .'
       '. . . the paint had gone, had cracked, had peeled off . . .'
Find all such sequences in this text.

4 What effect do you think these repetitions have?

5 Practise reading aloud each of the sentences in which the repetitions occur.

6 Work in pairs. Look at these two sentences.
   'The surrender of her weary ghost to the keeping of stars and sea was stirring
like the sight of a glorious triumph. The masts fell just before daybreak, and
for a moment there was a burst and turmoil of sparks that seemed to fill with
flying fire the night patient and watchful, the vast night lying silent upon the
sea.'
In these two sentences the narrator moves abruptly from the visionary (weary
ghost/glorious triumph) to the visual (masts/sparks). Consider how you would
read these two sentences aloud and what changes you would make for the
opening of the second sentence.

7 Discussion point (for group work).
Do you consider this text 'emotive' or 'non-emotive'?
Can you find any reasons in the text why it would be one or the other?

Reading aloud VI

The last extract in this unit deals with humour, and is from *The Prime of Miss Jean
Brodie* by Muriel Spark. (The book has been made into a highly successful film.)
The setting is Edinburgh in the 1930s. Miss Brodie is a schoolmistress with
'advanced' ideas, anxious to break out of the traditional patterns of education of
the time. To many people she would seem eccentric, not least to the class of 10- and
11-year-old girls in her charge.

1 Read the following extract silently.

Often, that sunny autumn, when the weather permitted, the small girls took their lessons seated on three benches arranged about the elm.

'Hold up your books,' said Miss Brodie quite often that autumn, 'prop them up in your hand, in case of intruders. If there are any intruders, we are doing our history lesson . . . our poetry . . . English grammar.'

The small girls held up their books with their eyes not on them but on Miss Brodie.

'Meantime I will tell you about my last summer holiday in Egypt . . . I will tell you about care of the skin, and of the hands . . . about the Frenchman I met in the train to Biarritz . . . And I must tell you about the Italian paintings I saw. Who is the greatest Italian painter?'

'Leonardo da Vinci, Miss Brodie.'

'That is incorrect. The answer is Giotto, he is my favourite.'

Some days it seemed to Sandy that Miss Brodie's chest was flat, no bulges at all, but straight as her back. On other days her chest was breast-shaped and large, very noticeable, something for Sandy to sit and peer at through her tiny eyes while Miss Brodie on a day of lessons indoors stood erect, with her brown head held high, staring out of the window like Joan of Arc as she spoke.

'I have frequently told you, and the holidays just past have convinced me, that my prime has truly begun. One's prime is elusive. You little girls, when you grow up, must be on the alert to recognise your prime at whatever time of your life it may occur. You must then live it to the full. Mary, what have you got under your desk, what are you looking at?'

Mary sat lump-like and too stupid to invent something. She was too stupid ever to tell a lie; she didn't know how to cover up.

'A comic, Miss Brodie,' she said.

'Do you mean a comedian, a droll?'

Everyone tittered.

'A comic paper,' said Mary.

'A comic paper, forsooth. How old are you?'

'Ten, ma'am.'

'You are too old for comic papers at ten. Give it to me.'

Miss Brodie looked at the coloured sheets. '*Tiger Tim's* forsooth,' she said, and threw it into the waste-paper basket. Perceiving all eyes upon it she lifted it out of the basket, tore it up beyond redemption and put it back again.

'Attend to me girls. One's prime is the moment one was born for. Now that my prime has begun – Sandy, your attention is wandering. What have I been talking about?'

'Your prime, Miss Brodie.'

Muriel Spark: *The Prime of Miss Jean Brodie*

2 As in *Reading aloud I* above there will be clear changes within the text. Mark all sections where Miss Brodie actually speaks. Then identify sections where she is:
   a) engaging in teacher talk; using the conventional language of teacher–pupil interaction;
   b) being a visionary; imagining herself a philosopher; being like Joan of Arc;
   c) correcting a pupil;
   d) being sarcastic;
   e) being stern;
   f) gaining the attention of the pupils.

3 Consider which of the variables might predominate in each of these sections.

4 Work in groups of four.
   One student takes the part of the narrator, reading all that part of the text which is not direct speech. This will generally be soft, non-emotive and with a fairly low (and level) pitch. One student reads the part of Miss Brodie, varying the part according to the action indicated in 2 above. One student reads all the remaining direct speech, that is, all the children's parts. (Consider how 10-year-old girls might speak to a teacher, especially such a teacher as Miss Brodie.) The fourth student is the producer. He or she has the right to stop any of the readers and require the part to be spoken differently.
   Then change roles.

EXPLOITATION

Re-read 'The Village Schoolmaster' in Unit 3, *Ranking I*. What similarities does Miss Brodie have with the village schoolmaster? How do you think the village schoolmaster would talk to his pupils?
Make use of the eight variables, if necessary.
Which one, do you think, would be the better teacher? Why?

SUMMARY OF THE UNIT

1 We hope that this unit has given you a little more confidence in reading aloud and in the oral expression of your interpretation of a text.
2 It is clear from *Reading aloud III* above that how words are said is crucial in drama. There is another extract from *Macbeth* to practise on (see Unit 2, *Scenario II*), but a very useful development would be to extend this approach to a reading of Pinter's *Last to Go* (see Unit 2, *Scenario III*).
3 How things are said can and should be studied in relation to all texts and you should try to practise on as many of the texts printed in this book as possible. 'Ozymandias' (Unit 2, *Scenario I* and Unit 3, *Orientation*) is another poem where judgement of loud–soft, quick–slow could be significant.
4 Don't forget that our eight variables can be expanded if you wish; certain categories may need to be removed or amended in the light of your experience.

Unit 5   'On the inside': Writing and patterns of language

Introduction for the student

In this unit we will pay closer attention to the language and style of literary texts. We will look at how the way a text is written produces certain effects. One of the best ways of exploring these effects is for you to try to use similar patterns in your own writing. This should help you experience a text not from the outside but from the inside.

SECTION A

Orientation

Look at the picture below. What do you think it would feel like to go on a space journey? Make notes which describe your feelings. Compare your notes with those of another student. What do you agree on?

Language patterns I

1 Read the following text. It is by contemporary British poet, Edwin Morgan, and was first published in 1966. As you start your reading, you will have to take some decisions. Will you read down the page with a pause between each list of words? If you decide to read across the page will you read the items from both columns with the same intonation? The reader on the cassette has had to make a decision. Read the text aloud to yourself and then compare your version with the one recorded on the cassette.

'*Spacepoem 3: Off Course*'

the golden flood   the weightless seat
the cabin song   the pitch black
the growing beard   the floating crumb
the shining rendezvous   the orbit wisecrack
the hot spacesuit   the smuggled mouth-organ   5
the imaginary somersault   the visionary sunrise
the turning continents   the space debris
the golden lifeline   the space walk
the crawling deltas   the camera moon
the pitch velvet   the rough sleep   10
the crackling headphone   the space silence
the turning earth   the lifeline continents
the cabin sunrise   the hot flood
the shining spacesuit   the growing moon
      the crackling somersault   the smuggled orbit   15
      the rough moon   the visionary rendezvous
      the weightless headphone   the cabin debris
      the floating lifeline   the pitch sleep
      the crawling camera   the turning silence
      the space crumb   the crackling beard   20
      the orbit mouth-organ   the floating song

Edwin Morgan

2 It is difficult to decide in which 'direction' to read the poem for a number of reasons. The first of these is probably the absence of punctuation and the second the absence of a main verb. What results from these unusual absences? Make a list of the difficulties caused by these aspects of the poem and ask yourself why the poet writes in this way.

Punctuation	*Reason*
a) No capital letters.	Because ....
b) No full stops.	Because ....
c) No commas or semi-colons.	Because ....

Grammar	Result
a) No main verbs.	*Example:* The reader does not know which words are subjects and which are objects. Verbs usually provide links. Therefore, the reader ....
b) If there are no main verbs then there is no tense. We do not have any sense of time.	The reader ....
c) No personal pronouns.	....
d)	....
e)	....

3 It is probably not quite true to say there are no verbs in the poem. There are several participles which are formed from verbs. List them before we go on to discuss their function.

4 What is the function of the present participle (e.g. 'floating') in English? For example, what is the difference in effect between the following?
   The space-ship floats in outer space.
   The floating space-ship in outer space.

5 Is 'the floating song' a fitting end to the poem? Why (not)?

6 There are interesting patterns in the poem. Chief among these are the repetitions of words. Work with a partner and list all the repetitions you can find. For example:
   l.2 the cabin song   l.21 the floating song
   l.11 the crackling headphone   l.15 the crackling somersault
   l.17 the weightless headphone

   ....
   ....

7 What do you notice about the patterns? How do the repeated words combine? What is the effect of these combinations? Make some preliminary notes.

8 Note the following sets of repeated items:
   l.2 the pitch black   l.18 the pitch sleep
   l.5 the smuggled mouth-organ l.21 the orbit mouth-organ
   l.7 the space debris   l.17 the cabin debris
   l.11 the crackling headphone l.17 the weightless headphone
   l.8 the golden lifeline   l.18 the floating lifeline

   Why is there a new paragraph / change of course or direction at line 15? Look closely at the above pairings of the words before and after line 15. Find more for yourself. What do you think has happened to the space ship or the 'journey' to which these lists of words seem to refer?

9 Discuss with another student any features of the shape of the poem or the language used by the poet which you find particularly striking. Make a list of points. Compare your list with those of others in your group.

10 Why do you think the poem has the title 'Off Course'?

EXPLOITATION

1 Write a paragraph explaining the relationship between the subject matter of this poem and the shape of the words printed on the page. The poem is by the seventeenth-century English poet, George Herbert.

> *Easter wings*
>
> Lord, who createdst man in wealth and store,
>   Though foolishly he lost the same,
>   Decaying more and more,
>   Till he became
>   Most poore: 5
>   With   thee
>   O let me rise
>   As larks, harmoniously,
>   And sing this day thy victories:
> Then shall the fall further the flight in me.   10
>
>   My tender age in sorrow did beginne:
>   And still with sicknesses and shame
>   Thou didst so punish sinne,
>   That   I   became
>   Most thinne.   15
>   With   thee
>   Let me combine
>   And feel this day thy victorie:
>   For, if I imp my wing on thine,
> Affliction shall advance the flight in me.   20
>
>   George Herbert

2 Now write a poem yourself using the following features of language and form:
   a) no punctuation;
   b) no main verb;
   c) a structure of *d a n* (where *d* = definite article, *a* = adjective, *n* = noun).

Be sure to make the reader see a connection between the shape in your poem and the subject matter. (Notice for example how the capital letters in the following poem are used to suggest the steps leading to the top of the tower.) This poem is an example of what can be done. It is a 'poem without a title' written by a Japanese student of English. When you have read the poem give it a title. The arrows were supplied by the student to show the 'direction' in which it is to be read.

The stone top

The damp echo

The cold wind

The held breath

The fading foothills   5

The small trees

The missed turning

The hopeless face

The chinks of light

The life-line sky   10

The greening moss

The cold echo

The stone steps

The lost recourse

The pelting rain   15

The howling winds

The stone tower   The stone body

3 How suitable do you think the following titles are?
  Which do you prefer?
    Suicide
    Cold Feeling
    The Tower and The Stone Body

4 Here is another poem written to the same model by an Italian adult student of
   English. Why is it written in a circle?

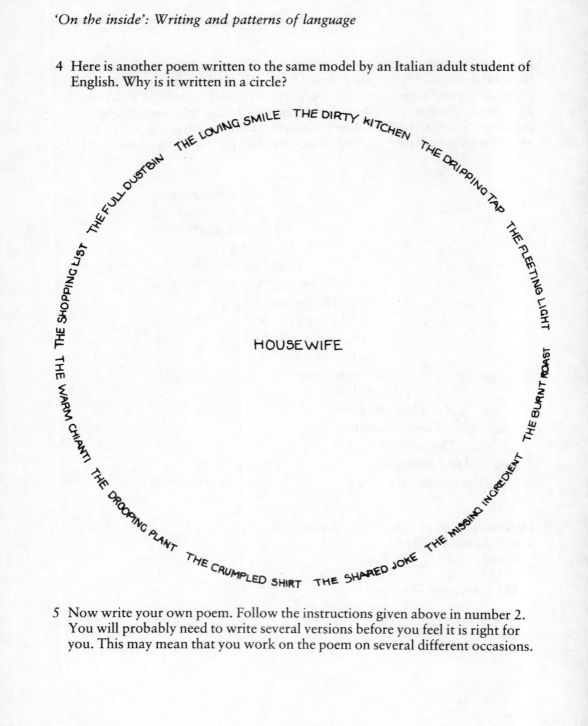

THE LOVING SMILE THE DIRTY KITCHEN THE DRIPPING TAP THE FLEETING LIGHT THE BURNT ROAST THE MISSING INGREDIENT THE SHARED JOKE THE CRUMPLED SHIRT THE DROOPING PLANT THE WARM CHIANTI THE SHOPPING LIST THE FULL DUSTBIN

HOUSEWIFE

5 Now write your own poem. Follow the instructions given above in number 2.
   You will probably need to write several versions before you feel it is right for
   you. This may mean that you work on the poem on several different occasions.

Language patterns II

1 Read the following poem. (See also Unit 2 *Orientation*.)

 *

   Meeting at Night

The grey sea and the long black land;
And the yellow half-moon large and low;
And the startled little waves that leap
In fiery ringlets from their sleep,
As I gain the cove with pushing prow,   5
And quench its speed i' the slushy sand.

Then a mile of warm sea-scented beach;
Three fields to cross till a farm appears;
A tap at the pane, the quick sharp scratch
And blue spurt of a lighted match,   10
And a voice less loud, thro' its joys and fears,
Than the two hearts beating each to each!

Robert Browning

2 Write a brief summary (no word limit) of (a) what you think happens and (b) what you think the poem is about. Pay attention in your summaries to the title. Why is it 'Meeting at Night' and not '*The* Meeting at Night' or '*A* Meeting at Night'? Consider why the voice expresses 'joys *and* fears'. Why is it '*at Night*'?

3 Notice that again we have a poem with no main verb and thus no main clause. This time, however, there are subordinate clauses '. . . As I gain the cove', '. . . till a farm appears'. Re-write the text and substitute a main finite verb. For example:
   I see and hear the grey sea and the long black land

   ....

   ....
   As I gain the cove ....
Do the same again with the next stanza.

4 What changes occur when you put in the main clauses? Read the poem again. Why do you think Browning wrote so many noun phrases in succession? What kind of effect does this produce on the reader? Check your summaries to see whether you made any reference to these effects.

5 In this section we shall turn away from grammar briefly to examine the sound structure of the poem. Now listen to the reading of this poem on the cassette, paying particular attention to the sounds the words create. What do you notice to be the main sounds in the poem? What is the effect of these sounds?

* The recording is to be found within Unit 2.   ⟫→

71

6 Read the poem again and examine its vowel sounds. Write out the poem on a piece of paper and, as you do so, mark the long and the short vowel sounds. For example:

    S   L L S S   S   S
    The grey sea and the long black land
    S   S SL(?) L   L   L S   L
    And the yellow half-moon large and low . . .

As you do this try also to work out which vowels are emphasised. Listen to the recording again if necessary. Do you agree with our analysis? Work out the alternation between short and long vowels in the poem. At what points (i.e. what is happening in the poem) is there a concentration of (a) long vowels and (b) short vowels? Do you think the rhythms of the poem are suited to the subject matter? Do you see any connection between the rhythm of the poem and the grammatical structures Browning uses? What is the connection between the language used and the feelings expressed?

Language patterns III

1 Look at the picture of the eagle below. What kind of bird is an eagle? Is it a powerful bird? How big are most eagles? How would you feel if you were close up to this bird? How would you react to seeing it fly?

2 The next poem is by a contemporary of Robert Browning's, Alfred Lord Tennyson. We shall return to this poem in Unit 6. The main point here is to ask you to consider just one feature of its grammar.

*

THE EAGLE

Fragment

He clasps the crag with crooked hands;	(a)
Close to the sun in lonely lands,	(a)
Ring'd with the azure world, he stands.	(a)
The wrinkled sea beneath him crawls;	(b)
He watches from his mountain walls,	(b)
And like a thunderbolt he falls.	(b)

Alfred Lord Tennyson

The poem is written in one tense throughout. What is it?
Why has Tennyson given such prominence to this tense?
To help you answer this question, try working through the following tasks:
a) Re-write the verbs in the simple past tense and ask yourself what happens to the way we see the eagle.
b) Re-write the verbs in the present continuous tense, for example, 'He *is clasping* . . .' What changes occur in our view of the subject?
In other words what is the function of this simple present tense? To help you consider this, examine the differences in meaning between the following:
i) Mr Jones is living in London.
   Mr Jones lives in London.
ii) The oil is floating on the water.
   Oil floats on water.
Now re-read the poem and write two or three sentences in answer to the question underlined at the beginning of this section.

3 Notice also the repetition of the third person pronoun in its different forms 'he', 'his', 'him'. Why is this repeated so often and what effect does the unusual word order create? For example, what different effects (irrespective of rhyme) would be produced if the final two lines were:
   He watches from his mountain walls
   And he falls like a thunderbolt.

4 Why do you think Tennyson has created a pattern of three rhyming words at the end of each line of each stanza (i.e. aaa/bbb)?
Look closely at the rhyme scheme employed by Browning in 'Meeting at Night'. What would have been the effect if Browning had used a pattern such as aaa/bbb/ccc/ddd or even aa/bb/cc?

EXPLOITATION

1 Imagine you are in a strange town. You are staying with friends and you are on your way back to their home. You are very tired and want to go to sleep. You lose your way. It is very dark and there are no lights. Clouds hide the moon. It

---

* The recording is to be found within Unit 6.   73

has just rained very heavily and there is mud everywhere. List, in note form, six main impressions you have. For example:
a) can't see where I'm going
b) people bump into me
c) slippery
d) ....
e) ....
f) ....

2 What are your feelings as you walk through this town? Are you irritated, angry, afraid, determined; or ... ?

3 Read the following extract from the opening to Dickens' novel *Bleak House*.

LONDON. Michaelmas Term lately over, and the Lord Chancellor sitting in Lincoln's Inn Hall. Implacable November weather. As much mud in the streets, as if the waters had but newly retired from the face of the earth, and it would not be wonderful to meet a Megalosaurus, forty feet long or so, waddling 5 like an elephantine lizard up Holborn Hill. Smoke lowering down from chimney-pots, making a soft black drizzle, with flakes of soot in it as big as full-grown snowflakes—gone into mourning, one might imagine, for the death of the sun. Dogs, undistinguishable in the mire. Horses, scarcely better; splashed to their very 10 blinkers. Foot passengers, jostling one another's umbrellas, in a general infection of ill-temper, and losing their foot-hold at street-corners, where tens of thousands of other foot passengers have been slipping and sliding since the day broke (if this day ever broke), adding new deposits to the crust upon crust of mud, 15 sticking at those points tenaciously to the pavement, and accumulating at compound interest.

Fog everywhere. Fog up the river, where it flows among green aits and meadows; fog down the river, where it rolls defiled among the tiers of shipping, and the waterside pollutions of a great (and 20 dirty) city. Fog on the Essex Marshes, fog on the Kentish heights. Fog creeping into the cabooses of collier-brigs; fog lying out on the yards, and hovering in the rigging of great ships; fog drooping on the gunwales of barges and small boats. Fog in the eyes and throats of ancient Greenwich pensioners, wheezing by the firesides of 25 their wards; fog in the stem and bowl of the afternoon pipe of the wrathful skipper, down in his close cabin; fog cruelly pinching the toes and fingers of his shivering little 'prentice boy on deck. Chance people on the bridges peeping over the parapets into a nether sky of fog, with fog all round them, as if they were up in a 30 balloon, and hanging in the misty clouds.

Gas looming through the fog in divers places in the streets,

much as the sun may, from the spongey fields, be seen to loom by husbandman and ploughboy. Most of the shops lighted two hours before their time—as the gas seems to know, for it has a haggard   35
and unwilling look.

    The raw afternoon is rawest, and the dense fog is densest, and the muddy streets are muddiest, near that leaden-headed old obstruction, appropriate ornament for the threshold of a leaden-headed old corporation: Temple Bar. And hard by Temple Bar, in   40
Lincoln's Inn Hall, at the very heart of the fog, sits the Lord High Chancellor in his High Court of Chancery.

Charles Dickens: *Bleak House*

4 What are the main impressions you get when you read this passage? Which words give you these feelings?

5 Notice that Dickens writes the three opening paragraphs without a main finite verb, for example: *Dogs, undistinguishable in the mire . . . Fog everywhere . . . fog down the river, where it rolls defiled among the tiers of shipping, and the waterside pollutions of a great (and dirty) city.*
  What is the main effect on the reader of sentences constructed in this way?

6 Return to your notes for 1 and 2. Without using a main finite verb, write a short paragraph in which you describe your imagined experiences in this town at night.

7 What is the effect of your grammar on the way you have put the words and experiences together?

8 In the final paragraph from the opening of *Bleak House* the main finite verbs are in the simple present tense. Why? What has changed in the description?

SECTION B

Orientation: Elastic sentences

In this section we shall use a technique we call 'elastic sentences'. For this you re-write a sentence making it longer or shorter. Experiencing for yourself how something is written should help you to work out the effect the writer is aiming at (e.g. using syntax and particular sentence patterns to create a certain style).

Here are two sentences. Combine them to make one sentence.
a) The man walked down the street.
b) The man met a friend.
This can be done in several ways. For example:

– The man met a friend as he walked down the street.
– The man walked down the street and met a friend.
– Walking down the street, . . .
Here are five sentences. Combine them to make one sentence. There are several ways it can be done.
a) The man walked down the street.
b) The man was wearing a black hat.
c) The hat was a bowler hat.
d) The man met a friend.
e) The friend was Japanese.
For example:
   The man, who was wearing a black bowler hat, walked down the street and met a Japanese friend.

Language patterns IV

1 Imagine you are in a big city. You have never been there before. You are on your way to meet someone you have not seen for a long time. You are excited about the meeting. There are lots of people everywhere and new sights and sounds all around you. Write a short paragraph or notes on what you imagine your impressions will be. Try and mix mental and visual impressions as much as possible.

2 The next extract is from the novel *Mrs Dalloway* by Virginia Woolf. Virginia Woolf's style is often thought to be difficult to read even by native speakers, so do not worry if everything is not clear at once. Read the passage.

> And for a second she wore a look of extreme dignity standing by the flower shop in the sunlight while the car passed at a foot's pace, with its blinds drawn. The Queen going to some hospital; the Queen opening some bazaar, thought Clarissa.
>
> The crush was terrific for the time of day. Lords, Ascot, Hurlingham, what was it? she wondered, for the street was blocked. The British middle classes sitting sideways on the tops of omnibuses with parcels and umbrellas, yes, even furs on a day like this, were, she thought, more ridiculous, more unlike anything there has ever been than one could conceive; and the Queen herself held up; the Queen herself unable to pass. Clarissa was suspended on one side of Brook Street; Sir John Buckhurst, the old Judge, on the other, with the car between them (Sir John had laid down the law for years and liked a well-dressed woman) when the chauffeur, leaning ever so slightly, said or showed something to the policeman, who saluted and raised his arm and jerked his head and moved the omnibus to the side and the car passed through. Slowly and very silently it took its way.

5

10

15

Clarissa guessed; Clarissa knew of course; she had seen   20
something white, magical, circular, in the footman's hand, a
disc inscribed with a name,—the Queen's, the Prince of
Wales's, the Prime Minister's?—which, by force of its own
lustre, burnt its way through (Clarissa saw the car diminishing,
disappearing), to blaze among candelabras, glittering stars,   25
breasts stiff with oak leaves, Hugh Whitbread and all his
colleagues, the gentlemen of England, that night in Bucking-
ham Palace. And Clarissa, too, gave a party. She stiffened a
little; so she would stand at the top of her stairs.

The motor car with its blinds drawn and an air of inscrutable   30
reserve proceeded towards Piccadilly, still gazed at, still
ruffling the faces on both sides of the street with the same dark
breath of veneration whether for Queen, Prince, or Prime
Minister nobody knew. The face itself had been seen only once
by three people for a few seconds. Even the sex was now in   35
dispute. But there could be no doubt that greatness was seated
within; greatness was passing, hidden, down Bond Street,
removed only by a hand's-breadth from ordinary people who
might now, for the first time and last, be within speaking
distance of the majesty of England, of the enduring symbol of   40
the state which will be known to curious antiquaries, sifting the
ruins of time, when London is a grass-grown path and all those
hurrying along the pavement this Wednesday morning are but
bones with a few wedding rings mixed up in their dust and the
gold stoppings of innumerable decayed teeth. The face in the   45
motor car will then be known.

It is probably the Queen, thought Mrs Dalloway, coming out
of Mulberry's with her flowers: the Queen.

Virginia Woolf: *Mrs Dalloway*

Part of the difficulty is that we move in and out of Clarissa's mind as she walks
through London and thinks she sees the Queen. We are given her thoughts and
what she sees as well as her thoughts about what she sees. The style of writing is
quite dense and complex in places.

3 We suggest that re-writing can help you to understand what elements produce a
style like this. Again you should try to write some 'elastic sentences'. It is best
done with a partner. This time you are asked to make the sentences shorter.
Practise on the following piece of prose before working on the extract from *Mrs
Dalloway*. Notice that in reducing sentences you regularly have to insert
pronouns or repeat noun phrases or replace deleted verbs or insert
demonstratives such as 'this' or 'these'.

⋙→

Sentence 1

a) James Bond, with two double bourbons inside him, sat in the final departure lounge of Miami airport and thought about life and death.

b) James Bond had two double bourbons inside him.
He sat in the final departure lounge of Miami airport.
He thought about life and death.

Sentence 2

a) A capungo is a bandit who will kill for as little as forty pesos, which is about twenty-five shillings – though probably he had been paid more to attempt the killing of Bond – and, from the look of him he had been an instrument of pain and misery all his life.

b) – A capungo is a bandit.
– A capungo (He) will kill for as little as forty pesos.
– Forty pesos (This) is about twenty-five shillings.
– ....
– ....

4 Continue to work in pairs and take any long sentence of five lines or more from the passage and re-write it to produce as many single main clauses as possible.

5 Repeat the exercise on another long sentence from the passage.

6 Compare your re-written sentences with the original sentences you selected from Virginia Woolf. What are the differences in style and impact? Try to work out what makes Virginia Woolf's style like this.

7 Notice the number of references to Clarissa Dalloway's thoughts. We are given a lot of information about what she is thinking as well as what she is seeing. Through her, we receive a rapid series of impressions. How far is this reflected in the syntax in this passage? In places like this, critics describe Virginia Woolf's style as a 'stream of consciousness'.

Language patterns V

1 Examine the following poem by Browning entitled 'Summum Bonum' in the light of the work you have done in this unit. Work in pairs and make notes on the effects of:
   a) the shape of the poem on the page;
   b) the repetition of structures – both syntactic and phonetic;
   c) the absence of a main verb;
   d) the use of rhyme;
   e) the tense, especially the past tense in the final lines.

All the breath and the bloom of the year in the bag of one bee:
   All the wonder and wealth of the mine in the heart of one gem:
In the core of one pearl all the shade and the shine of the sea:
   Breath and bloom, shade and shine,—wonder, wealth, and—
                      how far above them—
        Truth that's brighter than gem,
        Trust that's purer than pearl,—
Brightest truth, purest trust in the universe—all was for me
        In the kiss of one girl.

2 Compare your work here with an examination of similar patterns of language used by Browning in his poem 'Meeting at Night' (see *Language patterns II* above). See also Unit 2 *Orientation*.

EXPLOITATION

Here are some further models of poems for you to experiment with. Again the patterns are fairly simple in structure. Write your own poems along these lines.

Thin Poems

Only two words per line are allowed. Where possible there should be a predominant sound ('S' in this example) but the main aim is to write a text which is long and thin. For example:

    A Day By the Sea

    Slippery sand
    Crunchy shells

    Children shrieking
    Sinking toes

    Castles rise   5
    Feet stamp

    Salmon 'sarnies'
    Sticky fingers

    Seaweed slimy
    Fishy jelly   10

    Stoney beaches
    Shattered wooddrift

    Slushing waves
    Slapping pools

    Sun sleeps   15
    Empty chairs

Syllable Poems

What are the 'rules' for this type of poem? (There is a clue in what they are called.)
Try and write some yourself. What kind of topics lend themselves to this particular
'shape' of poem?

> *Going Home*
>
> Clang
> Bell rings
> People stand
> Many voices
> Children packing books   5
> Feet are trudging
> Going home
> Happy
> Now

Haiku

A haiku is a poem which is structured from 17 syllables with a pattern of:
    line 1 = 5
    line 2 = 7
    line 3 = 5
It may take several versions before you are satisfied with your final version of the
poem.

i)   Those wavering trees,
             How they beckon in the wind!
             I cannot follow.

ii)   A young, naked girl
             Is combing out her long hair
             Watched by an old moon.

SUMMARY OF THE UNIT

1 This unit has explored certain patterns of language in literary texts. We have
adopted a method of encouraging you to use such patterns in your own writing.
We hope that this writing will enable you to explore for yourself some effects of
such patterns of language.
2 Writing according to prescribed patterns is not easy but it can be improved with
practice. We hope for two things here. First, that you understand that good
writing is disciplined. It works within defined structures of language. Even if
writers sometimes break with structures for particular effects, they start working
with the basic patterns and structures of English. Totally 'free' writing is rarely

effective. Second, we hope that you have enjoyed your writing, especially the poems, and that you will go on to write more poems.

3 We hope you will want to find more poems to read by some of the writers you have begun to explore. Edwin Morgan, for example, has written several volumes of very varied poems. Another 'concrete' poet you may find interesting is Ian Hamilton Findlay.

4 We have concentrated here on some features of grammar and on the pattern of the words on the page. One of the poems, 'The Eagle', is studied again for its vocabulary in Unit 6.

Unit 6   Words and their impact: Structures of vocabulary

Introduction for the student

We begin this unit by considering some aspects of the structure of English vocabulary. Our prime concern here will not be the meaning of words; we leave up to you how much you interpret from the context and how much you look up in a dictionary. We concentrate instead on *how* words carry meaning.

In this unit we encourage you to explore how words in a language relate to each other. They are not isolated units although this is how they seem on the printed page. They are related to each other grammatically, and how they have meaning depends on what grammatical choices a writer makes (see Unit 5). Words are also related to each other; they belong to word families.

SECTION A

Orientation: Word families, strengths and scales

The first exercise is a simple one. It is designed to accustom you to the idea of vocabulary structure. We shall then go on to look at the use writers can make of *word families*.

1 Fill in the following two charts. Put a tick √ or cross X according to whether you think the information at the top of the columns is true or false.

Insects

	no. of legs*	can fly	dangerous to humans	frightening	eats other creatures
ant					
beetle					
butterfly					
wasp					

* Insert a number in this column

Wild Animals

	no. of legs*	can fly	dangerous to humans	frightening	eats other creatures
lion					
elephant					
snake					
giraffe					

Insects and wild animals do have common features but obviously insects are more closely related to each other than to wild animals. Now make up three short sentences which combine the attributes of the insects and wild animals in unusual ways. For example:

The snake jumped onto a branch and flew off.

The butterfly ate the elephant.

See what effects you can produce.

2 Now here are some words for big and small. Put stars next to the words according to how strongly you think the word denotes the quality to which it refers. We have begun the exercise for you. We will refer in future to *word strengths* in exercises of this type.

big	*small* ★
enormous ★★★	miniscule
colossal	petite
vast	microscopic
large ★	tiny
gigantic	minute ★★
monumental	diminutive

Again amusing effects can be produced by combining a very strong word with an object with contrasting features. For example:

A microscopic elephant.

A gigantic ant.

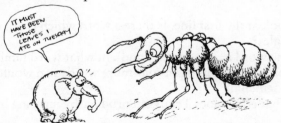

This kind of imaginative combination is particularly common in children's stories and also in the names of pop groups. Invent some names for pop groups and further combinations suitable for children's stories.

3 Finally, we want to introduce the idea of *word scales*. Here are four scales:

fast ————————————————————————— slow

small ———————————————————————— large

silent ——————————————————————— noisy

pleasant ——————————————————————unpleasant

Choose an insect and a wild animal from the charts in number 1 and put a cross on the scales for each one. Note that where you put the cross on the last scale is more subjective than on the others; that is, it depends much more on personal opinion.

Vocabulary I

1 Let us return to the poem by Tennyson 'The Eagle' (see also Unit 5, *Language patterns III*). Listen to how it is read on the cassette.

          THE EAGLE

Fragment

He clasps the crag with crooked hands;
Close to the sun in lonely lands,
Ring'd with the azure world, he stands.

The wrinkled sea beneath him crawls;
He watches from his mountain walls,   5
And like a thunderbolt he falls.

Alfred Lord Tennyson

2 Eagle: size (1)   speed (2)   strength (3)   noise (4)   guile (5)   attractiveness (6)

Which of these six qualities of the eagle are stressed most in the poem? Put your decisions in rank order, for example, 3 6 1 . . . and cite words from the poem to justify your choices.

3 Look at the first line. Is there a word which is not normally associated with eagles?
The word is, of course, 'hand'. In what word family does the word hand normally belong? List *four* more words you would connect with hand:
    arm, nail ....
What effect does Tennyson produce by merging bird-like and human qualities?

4 Now look at line 5. The poet links two words 'mountain' and 'wall'. Do they belong to the same word family? What words do you associate with 'mountain' and 'wall'? List them.

mountain	*wall*
sky	house
large	brick
high	small
....	....
....	....

5   Why does Tennyson link 'mountain' and 'wall'? Look closely at your lists of word families. Is it possible to imagine a house in the sky? Or a building with mountainous walls? Why do you think he has chosen the word 'watch' rather than 'see' or 'look'? Check closely the meaning of 'watch'. What is a 'watch-tower'? What links did you make? Compare them with another student's.

6   Where words from different word families are put together the result is what we call *metaphor*. Lines 1 and 5 are basically metaphoric. Line 6 also involves a comparison with the eagle. This time the eagle is compared to a 'thunderbolt'. The comparison is made quite openly and explicitly. (The term for this is a *simile*.) Again think of the features you would connect with a thunderbolt. Rate them on a scale:

silent _____ noisy

frightening _____ not frightening

Make up two more scales for 'thunderbolt'. Give them to another student to rate with a cross on the scale.

7   Now re-read the poem and write a paragraph on your interpretation of the poem. What does the eagle represent for you? Read the notes you made in your study in Unit 5, *Language patterns III*, before writing the paragraph.

EXPLOITATION

1   Now we would like you to create your own metaphoric effects. We will supply a word and you will make the comparison. As in the case of the eagle remember that there must be a clear connection between the object and the thing to which it is compared. Try to make the comparison an unusual and imaginative one.
a) The old man's face was wrinkled like ....
b) The clouds in the sky were white and fluffy like ....
    ....
c) The hungry dog was thin like ....

2   Now try filling two blanks:
a) Snow fell .... like ....
b) Her hair was .... like ....
c) The wind blows .... like ....
d) The snake crawls .... like ....

3 Form groups and decide which of the comparisons are the most effective. Give reasons for your choice.

4 Think about examples from *Vocabulary I*. How effective is the following line from Tennyson's 'The Eagle'? What image does the line conjure up?
'The wrinkled sea beneath him crawls'

Vocabulary II

1 Read the following description of a character and a building. It is taken from Chapter 21 of Dickens' novel *Great Expectations*. You worked on the first chapter of this novel in Unit 2.
Read the passage, noting the similes, metaphors and general comparisons of one thing to another.

He wore his hat on the back of his head, and looked straight before him, walking in a self-contained way as if there were nothing in the streets to claim his attention. His mouth was such a post office of a mouth that he had a mechanical appearance of smiling. We had got to the top of Holborn Hill before I knew that it was merely a mechanical appearance, and that he was not smiling at all. 5

"Do you know where Mr. Matthew Pocket lives?" I asked Mr. Wemmick.

"Yes," said he, nodding in the direction. "At Hammersmith, west of London." 10

"Is that far?"

"Well! Say five miles."

"Do you know him?"

"Why, you are a regular cross examiner!" said Mr. Wemmick, looking at me with an approving air. "Yes, I know him. *I* know him!" 15

There was an air of toleration or depreciation about his utterance of these words that rather depressed me; and I was still looking sideways at his block of a face in search of any encouraging note to the text, when he said here we were at Barnard's Inn. My depression was not alleviated by the announcement, for I had supposed that establishment to be a hotel kept by Mr. Barnard, to which the Blue Boar in our town was a mere public-house. Whereas I now found Barnard to be a disembodied spirit, or a fiction, and his inn the dingiest collection of shabby buildings ever squeezed together in a rank corner as a club for tom-cats. 20 25

We entered this haven through a wicket-gate, and were disgorged by an introductory passage into a melancholy little square that looked to me like a flat burying-ground. I thought it had the most dismal trees in it, and the most dismal sparrows, and 30 the most dismal cats, and the most dismal houses (in number half a dozen or so) that I had ever seen. I thought the windows of the sets of chambers into which those houses were divided were in every stage of dilapidated blind and curtain, crippled flower-pot, cracked glass, dusty decay, and miserable makeshift; while To Let To Let To Let glared at me from empty rooms, as if no new wretches ever came there, and the vengeance of the soul of Barnard were being slowly appeased by the gradual suicide of the present occupants and their unholy interment under the gravel. A frowzy mourning of soot and smoke attired this forlorn creation of Barnard, and it had strewed ashes on its head, and was undergoing penance and humiliation as a mere dust-hole. Thus far my sense of sight; while dry rot and wet rot and all the silent rots that rot in neglected roof and cellar—rot of rat and mouse and bug and coaching-stables near at hand besides—addressed themselves faintly to my sense of smell, and moaned, "Try Barnard's Mixture."

So imperfect was this realization of the first of my great expectations that I looked in dismay at Mr. Wemmick. "Ah!" said he, mistaking me, "the retirement reminds you of the country. So it does me."

Charles Dickens: *Great Expectations*

2 Write a short paragraph on Dickens' use of vocabulary here in which you cover some of the following questions:
   a) 'His mouth was such a post office of a mouth that he had a mechanical appearance of smiling.' What is the effect of 'post office of a mouth'?
   b) Why are the words 'dismal' and 'rot' repeated so often?
   c) What is the effect of '*crippled* flower-pot' and '*addressed themselves* faintly to my sense of smell, and *moaned*, "Try Barnard's Mixture"'?
   d) List all the words which describe Barnard's Inn as if it were a person. Why does Dickens describe the building in this way?
   e) Do you think that London comes up to Pip's 'Expectations'?

EXPLOITATION

Re-read the description of Coketown from Dickens' *Hard Times*, Unit 3, *Ranking III*. What similarities do you notice in the way vocabulary is used in that passage and in this extract from *Great Expectations*?

SECTION B

Orientation: Collocation and gap-filling

So far in this unit we have looked at word families, how metaphors and similes work, and the strength of words and how this can be measured using word scales. We shall now examine vocabulary patterns and how writers can exploit them. One important feature in this is *collocation*, or how words occur together in natural language. In our discussion of collocation we shall be making wide use of *gap-filling*. This involves you in filling in gaps we have left in texts with suitable words. In making your choice you will have to consider the appropriate word family, the grammar, and the style of the passage.

Vocabulary III

1 Here is an extract from a modern English novel by Michael Frayn. It is entitled *A Very Private Life* and was first published in 1968.

> ONCE upon a time there .... a little girl called Uncumber.
> Uncumber will have a younger brother called Sulpice, and they
> will live with their parents in a house in the middle of the woods.
> There will be no windows in the house, because there will be
> nothing to see outside except the forest. While inside there will be   5
> all kinds of interesting things – strange animals, processions,
> jewels, battles, mazes, convolutions of pure shapes and pure
> colours – which materialise in the air at will, solid and brilliant
> and almost touchable. For this .... in the good ....
> days a long, long while ...., and it .... like that in   10
> people's houses then. So the sight of the mud and grimy leaves
> outside would scarcely be of much interest.
> Then again, windows might let the .... in, and no one
> would want the congenial atmosphere of the house contaminated
> by the stale, untempered .... of the forest, laden with dust   15
> and disease. From one year's end to the next they won't go
> outside, and the outside world won't come in. There will be no
> ....; all their food and medicine and jewellery and toys will
> be on tap from the mains – everything they could possibly require
> will come to the house through the network of pipes and tubes   20
> and wires and electromagnetic beams which tangle the forest.
> Out along the wires and beams their wishes will go back. Back, by
> return, ... the fulfilment of them.

Michael Frayn: *A Very Private Life*

2 Fill in the gaps in the above passage from the following selection of words. Note that some of the words can be used more than once.

a) was   e) new   i) will come   m) air
b) will be   f) old   j) will   n) need
c) ahead   g) is   k) pure   o) contacts
d) ago   h) past   l) cold

3 Consult the complete passage in *Appendix 5*. You will probably be surprised by the results. Discuss the effect of the words actually used by Frayn in the passage. Write two sentences about these effects and then exchange your sentences with another student. Discuss any differences in your sentences.

4 The word 'will' can have several grammatical functions. Discuss the meaning of the word in the following sentences.

a) She *will* fly to London on Monday.
b) He has a strong *will*. He *will* not do it.
c) He *willed* the victory of his team.
d) The president *will* not be elected the next time.
e) She *will* just sit there for hours.

Discuss the effect of the repetition of 'will' in the passage.

5 It is important to realise that, as in this example, words which are primarily grammatical words like 'will', 'can' and 'should' can play a significant part in the overall structure of a text.

6 Before examining the next passage we would like you to try to imagine a village or small town in your own country which depends on a mine (coal, tin, diamond) for its existence. The majority of people work underground. What sort of buildings are there in this town? What do they look like? What are the schools like? What kind of entertainment do people have? Are the people likely to be rich or poor?

7 In this next passage from D. H. Lawrence's novel *Lady Chatterley's Lover* we have again deleted words. In the first ten lines you should choose from the list of words printed below the text. In the next 14 lines you have a clue in the form of the first letter of a word. In the remainder of the passage you have a completely free choice. Read the whole passage through carefully before you begin.

> The car .... uphill through the long squalid
> straggle of Tevershall, the blackened brick dwellings, the
> .... slate roofs glistening their sharp edges, the mud
> black with coal-dust, the pavements wet and .... It
> was as if dismalness had soaked through and through   5
> everything. The utter negation of natural beauty, the utter
> negation of the gladness of life, the utter absence of the instinct
> for shapely beauty which every bird and beast has, the

.... death of the human intuitive faculty was
.... The stacks of soap in the grocers' shops, the 10
rhubarb and lemons in the greengrocers! the awful hats in the
milliners! all went by ugly, ugly, ugly, followed by the
plaster-and-gilt horror of the cinema with its wet picture
announcements, 'A Woman's Love!', and the new big Primitive
chapel, p........................... enough in its stark brick and big panes 15
of greenish and raspberry glass in the windows. The Wesleyan
chapel, higher up, was of b........................... brick and stood
behind iron railings and b........................... shrubs. The Congregational chapel, which thought itself superior, was built of
rusticated sandstone and had a steeple, but not a very high one. 20
Just beyond were the new school buildings, expensive pink
brick, and gravelled playground inside iron railings, all very
i..........................., and mixing the suggestion of a chapel and a
p........................... . Standard Five girls were having a singing
lesson, just finishing the la-me-doh-la exercises and beginning 25
a 'sweet children's song'. Anything more unlike song, spontaneous song, would be impossible to imagine: a strange
bawling yell that followed the outlines of a tune. It was not like
savages: savages have subtle .... It was not like
animals: animals .... something when they 30
.... It was like nothing on earth, and it was called
....

D. H. Lawrence: *Lady Chatterley's Lover*

Words for lines 1–10:
  passed   progressed   ploughed   grey   dull   black   complete   thorough
  utter   awful   dreadful   appalling

8 Discuss the results of your gap-filling with another student. Justify your choices.
  Then work in larger groups (about 6–8) and vote to decide as a group which
  words should fill the gaps. Appoint a secretary who will read the passage which
  contains your final decisions to the class. He or she should be prepared to answer
  questions about your choices. The group should make sure the secretary knows
  the reasons for the choices.
  Lawrence's version is printed in *Appendix 6*.

SECTION C

Orientation: Lexical chains

In addition to word families and collocations it is of course possible to make long
lists of words which have associated meanings. Some of you may have tried this as

a game, either in the language learning classroom, or to pass the time on a boring journey. When you play the game, there has to be a logical connection between each word and the one that follows. For example:

post-office, post-box, mail, letter, stamp, collect, album etc.

The sequence could of course have developed quite differently. For example:

. . . letter, deliver, wait for, love . . .

If we made a circular instead of a horizontal pattern we could develop in different directions and take in a greater number of chains of words and ideas. Try this with the word 'THEATRE'.

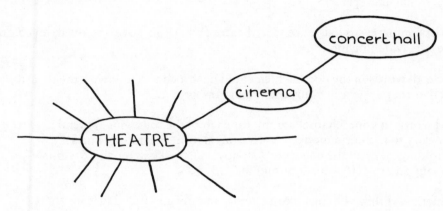

Develop one arm as follows: cinema → concert hall → opera house . . . ?

Develop other 'arms'. You are given only one or two words to begin each one:

a) stage, curtain . . .
b) audience, watch . . .
c) actor . . .
d) enjoy, laugh, applaud . . .
e) play, comedy . . .
f) box-office, ticket, book . . .
g) part, role . . .
h) costume, make-up . . .

We refer to this as a 'lexical chain diagram'.

When you think you have a nearly complete 'lexical chain diagram' for the word 'theatre' look at the poem below (see also Unit 1, *Prediction III*).

Vocabulary IV

> Of this world's theatre in which we stay,
> My love like the spectator idly sits
> Beholding me that all the pageants play,
> Disguising diversely my troubled wits.
> Sometimes I joy when glad occasion fits,   5
> And mask in mirth like to a comedy:

Soon after when my joy to sorrow flits,
I wail and make my woes a tragedy.
Yet she, beholding me with constant eye,
Delights not in my mirth nor rues my smart: 10
But when I laugh she mocks, and when I cry
She laughs and hardens evermore her heart.
What then can move her? if nor mirth nor moan,
She is no woman but a senseless stone.

Edmund Spenser

The poet compares his existence to a 'theatre', where his 'love' (beloved, loved one, fiancée) sits watching him.

1 Circle all words in the poem which could have a connection with the theatre, whether they appear in your 'chain diagram' or not.

2 Find words in your 'chain diagram' for each of the following (extend the 'arm' if necessary to include a modern word equivalent): 'spectator' (line 2); 'beholding' (3); 'all the pageants' (3); 'joy' (5); 'mask in mirth' (6); 'flits' (7); 'rues my smart' (10); 'mirth nor moan' (13).

3 'Sometimes I think I'm just like an actor, and my girl-friend just sits there watching me.'
Complete this paraphrase of the poem, trying to keep the same style ('I'm just like', 'my girl-friend just sits there'). Use your lexical chain diagram, and adapt it to the informal idiom where necessary.

4 Put a circle round 'My love' in line 2. Circle all other references to this person in the poem. Describe the lady without reference to the 'I' of the poem. Begin 'She's a hard woman. She watches every move he makes . . .'

5 Make a list of all the words which are repeated in the poem. Why do you think the poet repeats them?

6 List all the words in the poem connected with happiness. Why do you think there are so many? Do you think the poem is essentially happy or unhappy?

7 Many words in the poem have opposites, or antonyms. List these word pairs. What is the effect of so many positive words being cancelled by negative words?

8 What is the function of the word 'yet' (line 9)?

EXPLOITATION

1 Now we would like you to do some further work on the poem by Siegfried Sassoon called 'The General'. It was written during the First World War

1914–1918 (see Unit 9 for background). We studied it in Unit 4, *Reading aloud I*, where we examined how you would read it aloud. First re-read the text. It is printed on page 55.

2 Here we use two different word scales to help us work out the strength of three words from the poem. The aim is to help you to understand the meaning and tone of the words but also the attitude of the speaker towards the General. Much depends here on the tone and associations of the chosen words (see Unit 4, *Reading aloud I*).

3 Now study the words:
   curse   swine   slogged
Put stars against these words from one star ★ (weak) to three stars ★★★ (neutral) to five stars ★★★★★ (strong). The number of stars you use should show how powerfully you think the speaker feels about the object or activity in question.

4 Here is a scale. Rate the words along the scale. Do you think the words express positive (+) or negative (−) feelings?
   (+) ——————————————————————————————— (−)

5 Now rate these words in relation to other words that could be fitted into the context as alternatives. This will help you to work out the tone of the words in the poem.
   a) *curse*, complain about, grumble about
   b) *swine*, people, soldiers
   c) *slogged*, walked, marched

SUMMARY OF THE UNIT

1 This unit has shown how words link with each other in a literary text. They can belong to the same word family, they can be synonyms or antonyms and they can occur in usual or unusual combinations. The way the words are linked depends on the particular expressive aim of the writer.
2 We suggest that, if you spend all your time looking up words in a dictionary, you can miss this important point in reading literature. Please continue to use your dictionaries but don't feel you have to look up every word. The pattern of words can be equally important to the meaning of the poem and the effect it makes on you.
3 Vocabulary is important. But it is not everything. You can see this if you compare your work here on vocabulary in 'The Eagle' with your work on other patterns of language in the poem in Unit 5. The total meaning of words in a poem dictates how to read them aloud (see Unit 4). When we read a poem aloud it also gives us a chance to indicate the strength of a word. Sassoon's 'The General' (see also Unit 4, *Reading aloud I*) is a good example of this.
4 The extract from *Lady Chatterley's Lover* which describes the village of Teborghall (see *Vocabulary III*) is studied again in Unit 7, page 103.

Unit 7 Re-writing: Literary and non-literary discourse

Introduction for the student

In this unit we shall be examining some features of language which literary and non-literary texts share. Our aim is to help you to appreciate what makes some texts literature and understand how language is used to create certain effects in non-literary contexts. You will re-write texts in different styles for each exploitation exercise. This should enable you to analyse the language of different kinds of text, to focus on the effect the writer is aiming at and on how it is being achieved. Above all, we hope this unit will encourage you to read and enjoy all kinds of writing and to continue to explain why you enjoy what you enjoy.

Orientation

1 Read the following text.

A   Commence by replacing the hub-bearing outer race (33), Fig. 88, which is a press fit and then drop the larger bearing (32) into its outer member followed by the oil seal (31), also a press fit, with lip towards bearing. Pack lightly with grease.

   If the hub is to be fitted to a vehicle equipped with disc brakes, a   5
concentric ring of Prestic 5686 must be applied between the shield and axle face. On hubs with drum brakes, apply sealing compound between shield and back-plate.

   Fit hub (28) to stub axle (1) and fit the inner member of the outer race, also greased. Replace the inner nut (34) and tighten   10
to remove all end-float. If discs are fitted check run-out (see page 63). Slacken inner nut two holes and check end-float (0.004–0.006 in.) using a dial gauge.

2 Where would you expect to meet such language?

3 What gives you a clue that you need a diagram to help you to follow this text?

4 Why do you think so many of the words have a number after them (e.g. 'inner nut' (34))?

5 Why are so many of the verbs in the imperative mood (e.g. 'fit', 'apply', 'slacken', etc.)?

6 Do you think this text would be read for pleasure?

7 Discuss the following question with another student. Why are the words in this text so unambiguous?

8 Now read the following text.

B

> Have you had the great Sunday car washing ritual?
>
> Have you got better things to do with a car than run round it with a rag, and show it off to your neighbours? 5
>
> Then the Maxi is for you.
>
> Because the Maxi was made for doing things.
>
> In a Maxi, you can run your wife and kids around in real comfort.
>
> Or do 500 miles in a day without trouble, and save on your fuel bills. And if you have to take the odd pram, chicken coop or chest of drawers with you, you can do that, too. 10
>
> Just drop the rear seat flat and slide it in through the wide fifth door at the back. 15
>
> In the front, you've got two fully-reclining seats. Which will turn into a full size double bed, should you need it.
>
> You're not short of pulling power either. With a proven 1,485 cc. overhead cam transverse engine, a five-speed gear box and our famous front-wheel drive. 20

9 Work in pairs on the following questions:
   a) Why are there questions in this text? Think about this in comparison with text A above.
   b) Why is the personal pronoun 'you' used so much?

10 Where could you expect to meet such language? How would it be presented?

11 Look closely at the third sentence in the text: 'Then the Maxi is for you.' It comes after two questions. What effect does it create?

12 Why does the writer of the passage refer to 'our *famous* front-wheel drive'?

13 Read this text aloud. Is your attention drawn by any particular sequences of sounds? What is their effect?

14 Why is the word 'ritual' used? What is the connection between 'ritual' and 'Sunday'?

15 Analyse the first five sentences of this text. Pay attention to its stylistic patterns, grammar, phonology, vocabulary etc.

16 Could text A be patterned in the same way?

17 Now read the next text. It is a passage which also deals with motor cars.

C   A minute later Dixon was sitting listening to a sound like the ringing of a cracked door-bell as Welch pulled at the starter. This died away into a treble humming that seemed to involve every component of the car. Welch tried again; this time the effect was of beer-bottles jerkily belaboured. Before Dixon could do more   5 than close his eyes he was pressed firmly back against the seat, and his cigarette, still burning, was cuffed out of his hand into some interstice of the floor. With a tearing of gravel under the wheels the car burst from a standstill towards the grass verge, which Welch ran over briefly before turning down the drive.   10 They moved towards the road at walking pace, the engine maintaining a loud lowing sound which caused a late group of students, most of them wearing the yellow and green College scarf, to stare after them from the small covered-in space beside the lodge where sports notices were posted.   15

18 Do you think text C would normally be accompanied by a picture or a drawing? If so why? If not, why not?

19 Look closely at the way the writer makes comparisons:
    a) The starter sounded *like the ringing of a cracked door-bell*.
    b) The sound died away *into a treble humming*.
    c) The starter sounded *like beer-bottles jerkily belaboured*.
    d) The engine made *a loud lowing sound* ('low' is a sound associated with cattle).
    e) There was a *tearing* of gravel under the wheels of the car.
    Rank these in order of effectiveness.

20 The three texts above all describe motor cars. But they all convey the information in different ways and for different purposes. Which of the texts is the most informative? (Be careful to define just what you mean by

information.) Discuss in pairs such factors as who is writing for whom, what kinds of information are communicated and why information about the car is differently emphasised from one passage to the next.

Re-writing I

1 Now read the following two texts. Both ask the reader to look closely at what is in most countries a common household or office instrument.

A

1 Lift handset
Listen for dial tone. (Continuous purring or new dial tone – high-pitched hum).

2 Insert money
At least minimum fee. Credit display stops flashing on insertion of minimum fee.

Do not insert money for operators or SOS-Emergency (999) calls.

If dial tone stops before you start to dial, press blue follow-on call button, listen for dial tone, then dial number.

3 Dial number
Listen for ringing tone. Speak when connected.

Failed call? New call with remaining credit?
Do not replace handset. Press blue follow-on call button, listen for dial tone, then re-dial. (Minimum fee still applies. Insert more money if necessary.)

To continue a dialled call – when you see display flashing and hear paytone (rapid pips), or anytime during call, insert more money.

4 Replace handset
Value showing on credit display is not always returnable. Only wholly unused coins returned.

B   . . .
          In homes, a haunted apparatus sleeps,
          that snores when you pick it up.

          If the ghost cries, they carry it
          to their lips and soothe it to sleep

          with sounds. And yet, they wake it up   5
          deliberately, by tickling with a finger.

          Craig Raine: 'A Martian Sends a Postcard Home'

2 Like car text A (p. 94), there are many imperatives in telephone text A (e.g. 'lift', 'insert', 'dial', 'replace', 'listen' etc.). Why?

3 Text A above also makes use of different kinds of print. Why?

4 Why are there so many different paragraphs? What does the lay-out of the text contribute to the way we read it?

5 Now give some thought to how the lines are arranged in text B. Notice, for example, that the line regularly breaks with a verb or verb phrase and that the next line resumes with an adverb or adverbial phrase ('to their lips', 'with sounds', 'deliberately' etc.). What is the effect of the line break on the reader?

6 List all the words in the extract from the poem which are connected with sleep. Why is sleep a dominant image for the view of the telephone given by the Martian? Is it a good comparison?

7 Who is the 'they' in the third and fifth lines?

8 What is the point of the title of this poem?

9 Write a paragraph in which you explain the different purposes of each text. Consider some of the following points:
   a) Text A does not contain any metaphors or ambiguous words. Why not?
   b) If you read text A without a telephone in front of you or in your hand, would it matter?
   c) If you read text B without a telephone in front of you, would it matter?
   d) Why is the word 'telephone' not mentioned in text B?

EXPLOITATION

The poem in text B and others from the volume (from which this is the title poem) give a view of the world of everyday human objects and actions through the eyes of a complete stranger from another planet. Imagine you are a Martian. Write home short 'postcard' descriptions in either poetry or prose of two of the following:

a) a television;
b) a radio;
c) trying to start the engine of a very old car;
d) people in a swimming pool;
e) two people greeting each other (take one example from your own culture and then one from another culture you know of);
f) opening and drinking a bottle or can of Coca-Cola.

Re-writing II

1 We shall now turn our attention away from objects and on to places. Read the following extract from a description of Rome. Where would you expect to find such a description? Place the following in rank order from the most to the least likely:
a) a geography book;
b) a novel;
c) a history of Rome;
d) a guide book;
e) a holiday brochure.

ROME

Rome, the eternal city, is enriched by more than 2,500 years of history. There's no other city in the world with as many masterpieces of art and architecture – impressive ancient remains, as well as renaissance and baroque palaces, churches and monuments. Famous sights like the Colosseum, where gladiators fought and Christians were sacrificed to the lions and the Roman Forum, which was the commercial, civil and religious centre of Republican Rome, are still steeped in the atmosphere of ancient Rome. The Spanish steps, the Trevi Fountain and the Villa Borghese reveal the city's more recent glorious history. In the Vatican City, the smallest state in the world and the centre of the Roman Catholic faith is the Basilica of St. Peter, whose Sistine Chapel houses what is, perhaps, Michelangelo's greatest work – the massive sculptural forms of his painting which cover the entire ceiling. There's lots more to see – several networks of catacombs hollowed out by early Christians; the Pantheon; the Castel Sant'Angelo, Mausoleum of the Emperor Hadrian; the Protestant Cemetery where Keats and Shelley are buried and the Campidoglio, the Sacred Hill of ancient Rome. For evening entertainment there are numerous nightclubs, discotheques and bars and you'll find thousands of eating places. Many of the city's most fashionable shops, nightclubs and cafés are in and around the Via Veneto and Piazza di Spagna.

Accommodation: Hotel Delta, *T T T* or Residence Palace, *T T T*, both of which are near the Colosseum in the centre of Rome.

Prices shown are per person for bed and breakfast only in a room with two beds, with private bath and w.c. Supplements (per person per night): half board £5; single room (with shower instead of bath) £1.75.

2 Now look carefully at the following words and structures. Then look back at your ranking and see if you still wish to keep the same order.
   'There's no other city in the world with as many'
   'impressive ancient remains'
   'Famous'
   'more recent *glorious* history'
   'greatest work'
   'massive sculptural forms . . . cover the *entire* ceiling'
   'There's *lots more* to see'
   'most fashionable'

3 In your opinion, what do the words and phrases in italics have in common?

4 Why does the text begin to use the personal pronoun 'you' at the end?

5 Write a description of your own capital city in which you use some of the phrases underlined in number 2.

6 Check your ranking in number 2 with another member of your class and analyse where and why you agree or disagree.

7 The following extract is from George Eliot's novel *Middlemarch*. Dorothea Brooke, the heroine, has recently married Mr Casaubon, a man much older than herself and a scholar devoted to studies of the ancient world. They have come to Rome for their honeymoon. At home in England Dorothea idolised Mr Casaubon and his knowledge.

Two hours later, Dorothea was seated in an inner room or boudoir of a handsome apartment in the Via Sistina.
   I am sorry to add that she was sobbing bitterly, with such abandonment to this relief of an oppressed heart as a woman habitually controlled by pride on her own account and thoughtfulness for others   5
will sometimes allow herself when she feels securely alone. And Mr Casaubon was certain to remain away for some time at the Vatican.
   Yet Dorothea had no distinctly shapen grievance that she could state even to herself; and in the midst of her confused thought and passion, the mental act that was struggling forth into clearness was a self-accusing cry   10
that her feeling of desolation was the fault of her own spiritual poverty.

She had married the man of her choice, and with the advantage over most girls that she had contemplated her marriage chiefly as the beginning of new duties: from the very first she had thought of Mr Casaubon as having a mind so much above her own, that he must often   15
be claimed by studies which she could not entirely share; moreover, after the brief narrow experience of her girlhood she was beholding Rome, the city of visible history, where the past of a whole hemisphere seems moving in funeral procession with strange ancestral images and trophies gathered from afar.   20

But this stupendous fragmentariness heightened the dreamlike strangeness of her bridal life. Dorothea had now been five weeks in Rome, and in the kindly mornings when autumn and winter seemed to go hand in hand like a happy aged couple one of whom would presently survive in chiller loneliness, she had driven about at first with Mr   25
Casaubon, but of late chiefly with Tantripp and their experienced courier. She had been led through the best galleries, had been taken to the chief points of view, had been shown the greatest ruins and the most glorious churches, and she had ended by oftenest choosing to drive out to the Campagna where she could feel alone with the earth and sky, away   30
from the oppressive masquerade of ages, in which her own life too seemed to become a masque with enigmatical costumes.

George Eliot: *Middlemarch*

8 Who is the 'I' of the second paragraph?

9 Why does Dorothea now drive about less frequently with her husband?

10 Why does she prefer to drive out of the city and be alone?

11 Compare the use of the phrases 'the *best* galleries', 'the *greatest* ruins', 'the *most glorious* churches' with similar uses in the previous passage. Why does the author make such references here?

12 Why are the following comparisons made by the author?
    a) '... the past of a whole hemisphere seems moving in funeral procession';
    b) '... the dreamlike strangeness of her bridal life';
    c) '... her own life ... seemed to become a masque with enigmatical costumes'.

Re-writing III

Here are two more descriptions of places. The first text (A) is an encyclopaedia entry describing the country of Malaysia; the second (B) describes the reactions to Malaysia of one of the main characters, Doris, in the short story 'The Force of Circumstance' by Somerset Maugham. The story is studied in full in Unit 10.

A   *Malaysia, East, part of Federation of Malaysia*: inc. Sarawak and Sabah (formerly Brit. N. Borneo); less developed than W. Malaysia; p. concentrated on cst.; hill tribes engaged in hunting in interior; oil major exp., exploration off cst.; separated from W. Malaysia by S. China Sea; a. 77,595 sq. m.; p. (1968) 1,582,000.

Malaysia, Federation of, indep. federation (1963), S.E. Asia; member of Brit. Commonwealth; inc. W. Malaysia (Malaya) and E. Malaysia (Borneo sts. of Sarawak and Sabah); cap. Kuala Lumpur; a. 129,000 sq. m.; p. 1968) 10,455,000.

Malaysia, West (Malaya), part of Federation of Malaysia; consists of wide peninsula, S. of Thailand; most developed in W.; world's leading producer of natural rubber, grown in plantations; oil palm and pineapples also grown; world's leading exporter of tin; nearly half p. Chinese; a. 50,806 sq. m.; p. (1968) 8,899,000.

B   Of course she had read novels about the Malay Archipelago and she had formed an impression of a sombre land with great ominous rivers and a silent, impenetrable jungle. When the little coasting steamer set them down at the mouth of the river, where a large boat, manned by a dozen Dyaks, was waiting to take them   5
to the station, her breath was taken away by the beauty, friendly rather than awe-inspiring, of the scene. It had a gaiety, like the joyful singing of birds in the trees, which she had never expected. On each bank of the river were mangroves and nipah palms, and behind them the dense green of the forest. In the distance   10
stretched blue mountains, range upon range, as far as the eye could see. She had no sense of confinement nor of gloom, but rather of openness and wide spaces where the exultant fancy could wander with delight. The green glittered in the sunshine and the sky was blithe and cheerful. The gracious land seemed to   15
offer her a smiling welcome.

W. Somerset Maugham: 'The Force of Circumstance'

Work with another student and list five main differences in the way the places are described. Pay particular attention to style (e.g. grammar, vocabulary, patterns of sound, typographic layout etc.) in relation to the purpose of the passage. Would you, for example, expect to find the following phrases in an encyclopaedia entry:
     'a sombre land with great ominous rivers and a silent, impenetrable jungle'?
     'the sky was blithe and cheerful'?
Consider also why there are so many abbreviations in text A.
Would you expect Doris to record that Malaysia has a population of 10,455,000 and is the world's leading producer of natural rubber?
Why is the writer exploring Doris's responses?

EXPLOITATION

1 Read the following passage from D. H. Lawrence's *Lady Chatterley's Lover* in
  which the fictional mining village of Tevershall in England is described. You will
  probably have read the passage in your work on Unit 6, *Vocabulary III*.

> The car ploughed uphill through the long squalid straggle of
> Tevershall, the blackened brick dwellings, the black slate roofs
> glistening their sharp edges, the mud black with coal-dust, the
> pavements wet and black. It was as if dismalness had soaked
> through and through everything. The utter negation of natural   5
> beauty, the utter negation of the gladness of life, the utter
> absence of the instinct for shapely beauty which every bird and
> beast has, the utter death of the human intuitive faculty was
> appalling. The stacks of soap in the grocers' shops, the rhubarb
> and lemons in the greengrocers! the awful hats in the milliners!   10
> all went by ugly, ugly, ugly, followed by the plaster-and-gilt
> horror of the cinema with its wet picture announcements, 'A
> Woman's Love!', and the new big Primitive chapel, primitive
> enough in its stark brick and big panes of greenish and
> raspberry glass in the windows. The Wesleyan chapel, higher   15
> up, was of blackened brick and stood behind iron railings and
> blackened shrubs. The Congregational chapel, which thought
> itself superior, was built of rusticated sandstone and had a
> steeple, but not a very high one. Just beyond were the new
> school buildings, expensive pink brick, and gravelled play-   20
> ground inside iron railings, all very imposing, and mixing the
> suggestion of a chapel and a prison. Standard Five girls were
> having a singing lesson, just finishing the la-me-doh-la
> exercises and beginning a 'sweet children's song'. Anything
> more unlike song, spontaneous song, would be impossible to   25
> imagine: a strange bawling yell that followed the outlines of a
> tune. It was not like savages: savages have subtle rhythms. It
> was not like animals: animals *mean* something when they yell.
> It was like nothing on earth, and it was called singing.

> D. H. Lawrence: *Lady Chatterley's Lover*

2 Using the information given in the passage re-write it as either:
  a) an encyclopaedia entry (at least four lines) or
  b) a travel brochure (a short paragraph).
  You should use the styles of discourse illustrated on page 102 and page 99 as
  examples.

3 Re-read the passage by Lawrence. Which words or phrases express most clearly
  his attitudes towards Tevershall? In your re-writes have you expressed a view or
  an attitude towards the place? Why? Why not?

4 Now look at the following re-write of this passage as an estate agent's description, done by a student of English in Singapore.

Accommodation Available: Houses.

TEVERSHALL VICINTY. Brick dwellings with slate roofs and concrete pavements. Good location. Convenient to workers in the coal-mine. Easy access to such amenities as grocers' shops, greengroces' and milliners'. Recreational facilities include a cinema. For your religious requirements, there are the Primitive, Wesleyan and Congregational chapels. 5 mins drive to the new school buildings. Available for immediate occupation for both sale or lease at reasonable prices. Interested, call 492864.

Would you like to live in a place like Tevershall? If you had only read about the 'Accommodation Available' would you be tempted or not? What kind of pictures or photographs would you add to the description? Why are such photographs needed?

Re-writing IV

Here is another extract from 'The Force of Circumstance'. The description is now that of Guy, Doris's husband, the other main character in the story. This is how Doris 'sees' Guy early in the story.

A He was twenty-nine, but he was still a school-boy; he would never grow up. That was why she had fallen in love with him, perhaps, for no amount of affection could persuade her that he was good-looking. He was a little round man, with a red face like the full moon, and blue eyes. He was rather pimply.   5
. . .

104

He was a gay, jolly little man, who took nothing very solemnly, and he was constantly laughing. He made her laugh too. He found life an amusing rather than a serious business, and he had a charming smile. When she was with him she felt happy and good-tempered. And the deep affection which she saw in those 10
merry blue eyes of his touched her. It was very satisfactory to be loved like that.
. . .

It was hard to realize that nine months ago she had never even heard of him. She had met him at a small place by the seaside where she was spending a month's holiday with her mother. 15
Doris was a secretary to a member of parliament, Guy was home on leave. They were staying at the same hotel, and he quickly told her all about himself. He was born in Sembulu, where his father had served for thirty years under the second Sultan, and on leaving school he had entered the same service. He was devoted 20
to the country.

W. Somerset Maugham: 'The Force of Circumstance'

The following descriptions of Guy are in different styles and are written from different viewpoints and for different purposes. Where would you expect to find each one?

B

To Whom It May Concern

    I have known Guy Smith for five years. He
has worked under my direction in the Sultan's
service in Sembulu, Malaysia. Like his father
before him, Mr Smith has always worked
conscientiously and with enthusiasm. He is
devoted to his work. He has an infectiously
cheerful disposition and works well with his
colleagues. I recommend him to you highly.

C

Attention

W. Malaysia Police Force issue the
following description of a man
reported missing in the Sembulu
district. The man, Guy Smith, is in his
late twenties. He is below average 5
height, rotund in figure and has blue
eyes and a pimply complexion. He was
last seen wearing a pale blue shirt and
dark grey trousers. Anyone who has
seen this person or who has 10
information about his whereabouts
please contact Chief Inspector Robert
Sang at the Sembulu constabulary,
Tel: 07–41835.

Compare the above descriptions of Guy. In pairs write four questions which direct attention to the differences in style between the three descriptions. For example: Why would it be unusual to find the following sentence from text A in either text B or text C?

       'He had a charming smile.'

Join up with another pair. Answer their questions and let them answer yours. Make sure you are all satisfied with the answers.

EXPLOITATION

1 Read the following poem 'Reported Missing' by the contemporary British poet, Barry Cole.

Reported Missing

Can you give me a precise description?
Said the policeman. Her lips, I told him,
Were soft. Could you give me, he said, pencil
Raised, a simile? Soft as an open mouth,
I said. Were there any noticeable   5
Peculiarities? he asked. Her hair hung
Heavily, I said. Any particular
Colour? he said. I told him I could recall
Little but its distinctive scent. What do
You mean, he asked, by distinctive? It had   10
The smell of a woman's hair, I said. Where
Were you? he asked. Closer than I am to
Anyone at present, I said; level with
Her mouth, level with her eyes. Her eyes?
He said. What about her eyes? There were two,   15
I said, both black. It has been established
He said, that eyes cannot, outside common
Usage, be black; are you implying that
Violence was used? Only the gentle
Hammer blow of her kisses, the scent   20
Of her breath, the . . . Quite, said the policeman,
Standing, but I regret that we know of
No one answering to such a description.

Barry Cole

a) Someone close to you has gone missing. This can be a brother or sister, close friend or relative. You have to report their absence to the police. The first thing the police-officer asks you for is a physical description. Write a paragraph describing the missing person. Remember to write it in such a way that the individual will be recognised easily.

b) Now ask yourself some questions about your description: What are the differences in the kind of description by the 'poet' and the description you have produced for the police-officer? Did your description contain any metaphors? Why (not)? Did you convey your feelings about the person? Why (not)? What aspects of the missing person does the poet describe? Could anyone identify the missing person from the poet's description? Why (not)?

2 Look at the following airline advertisement and read carefully the character sketch of the pilot, Captain Thorstensen.

Meet Arne Thorstensen

Golfer. Yachtsman (29-footer). SAS DC-10 Captain. With 18,000 flying hours to his credit, Norwegian Arne Thorstensen epitomizes the experience and professionalism of SAS Flight Deck crews.

"Since joining SAS in 1949, I've flown most of the Douglas planes from the old DC-3 to our present wide-body DC-10s, now operating on Southeast Asia — and worldwide. After more than seven million miles as a commercial pilot, I know when passengers enjoy our service. I get the impression they like the Scandinavian shortcut to Europe. Certainly our four DC-10 flights per week offer a rather pleasant way to cross continents.

Welcome aboard!"

SAS
SCANDINAVIAN AIRLINES

Fly the Viking fleet to Copenhagen — and all around the world.

Imagine you are writing a novel in which Captain Thorstensen is one of the main characters. Introduce him to your readers in a short paragraph. Where possible, try to use some of the information given in the advertisement. Compare your results with another student's. What have you both left out and what have you included? Why?

SUMMARY OF THE UNIT

The nature of literary discourse is not easy to define and we have only described some of the more obvious linguistic features. In fact, we hope that you will see this unit as exploratory.

1 As we examine different styles of writing on a related theme or *re-write* a text in a different style, the different functions of literary and non-literary discourse can become clearer.
2 We also think that examining and producing for yourself different varieties of English is an important stage in improving your command of the language.
3 Literary texts exhibit some of the most skilful and moving uses of language. But all language requires careful manipulation and in some discourses, such as in advertisements, it can be quite 'literary' in places.

Unit 8   Under the microscope: Introduction to stylistic analysis

Introduction for the student

In the first part of this unit we shall look more closely at writers' choices of vocabulary. We begin with a gap-filling exercise, to prepare you for discussion of these choices. This type of exercise (see also Unit 6) is particularly useful because it involves you closely with these stylistic choices. We then use another technique, which we call 'scrambled sentences', to extend the work on 'patterns of language' and style done in Unit 5. In the final section of the unit we offer a detailed commentary on a poem by Thomas Hardy, examining the overall impact of the style of the poem. We advise you to read this commentary as well as the others in this unit several times. They should familiarise you with the kind of writing you might expect to find in books of literary criticism. This section brings together different aspects of style studied in previous units: grammar (Unit 5), vocabulary (Unit 6), sound patterns (Unit 4).

   The unit is designed primarily for self-access. It should help you to learn how to account for some of the complex effects writers can produce when they use language creatively. However, although we are putting the language of various texts under the microscope, you must be careful not to lose sight of the whole poem or piece of prose and your feelings and ideas about it.

SECTION A

Orientation: Gap-filling

Line 3 of 'Futility', which is the next poem we shall study, contains the words 'whispering of fields unsown'. This suggests that the soldier in the poem was a farmer and that during the war he left his fields at home unsown. If we read this line as a metaphor (see Unit 6, *Vocabulary 1*) it might suggest that he is a young man and has his whole life in front of him like a field which is still to be sown.

   Look at the picture on the next page. Imagine that the young man is to die soon. Do you know of anybody who has been killed at a young age, maybe as a teenager? Why is this especially tragic? Do you find it more or less tragic than the death of an old person or of a baby at birth? Is it more or less tragic if the death takes place during a war?

   Before reading the poem we suggest you read the account of the First World War

in Unit 9, *Background V*. 'Futility' was written by the poet Wilfred Owen who was an officer in the war and who was killed in battle in 1918. After reading the account, ask yourself why the word 'futile' might be used to describe wartime deaths?

Stylistic analysis I

1   In the text below there are several words missing. Read the poem carefully and then fill the gaps with a single word from the list of 12 alternatives for stanza 1 and 11 alternatives for stanza 2. You should try to put in the most likely word. This is not always an easy decision. Try to think of the word which will best fit with the surrounding words and pay attention to the grammar of the sentence in which that word appears. But don't forget that, as we saw in Unit 5, the success of a poem often depends on the overall pattern created by the words. Choose your word in relation to other words in the poem and the meanings they create. (Note that the first letter of two of the words is given as a clue.)

Futility

Move him into the .... —
Gently its touch awoke him once,
At home, whispering of fields unsown.
Always it woke him, even in France,
Until this morning and this snow.   5
If anything might r................. him now
The .... sun will know.

Think how it wakes the seeds,—
..............., once, the clays of a cold star.
Are limbs, so dear-achieved, are sides,   10
Full-nerved—still warm—too hard to ....?
Was it for this the .... grew tall?
—O what made f............... sunbeams toil
To break earth's sleep at all?

Wilfred Owen

Words for stanza 1:
early   shade   revive   old   restore   sun   morning   grave   kind   rouse
bright   hospital
Words for stanza 2:
youth   soldier   warmed   grass   futile   friendly   woke   move   clay
stir   fatuous

2 The next stage is to examine your choices for the first stanza in relation to
Owen's. The stars which break up the following discussion (★★★★★) mean you
should stop and give more time to your reading of the poem before going on.

Lines 1–7: Discussion

Line 1   There are a number of possible choices here. Knowing that the soldier is
seriously injured or (probably) dead we might put 'hospital' or 'grave'.
However it is not likely that there would be a hospital nearby and 'grave'
appears very final. Lines 6–7 seem to suggest that not all hope has been lost.
Grammatically, what does 'its touch' in line 2 refer back to? Try substituting
your choices. For example:
        'Gently the grave's touch awoke him once' (?)
and discuss how reasonable they seem. We might also want to move an
injured soldier's body into the 'shade'. But the reference to 'snow' in line 5
seems to suggest that it is warmth not cool shade the body needs. Owen
wrote:
        'Move him into the *sun*'
The choice also points forward to line 7 where 'sun' is mentioned again. The
stanza begins and ends with reference to the 'sun'. What associations do you
have with the sun? Consider whether this might change from one culture to
another and from one country to another. Remember that this is France in
winter and with snow on the ground.

Line 6   Here you are given a clue. The first letter is 'r'.
The sun will know how to r............... the soldier (who is very seriously,
perhaps mortally, wounded). What was your choice?
    revive?   restore?   rouse?
Owen wrote 'rouse'. What does the word mean? What is the word in this
stanza of which it is a synonym?

★★★★★

'Rouse' is an example of a word which has been selected because of the patterns it establishes with other words in the stanza. It is an example of assonance. That is, it has the same vowel sound as the word 'now'. But its main link is with 'wake'. This link seems stylistically important because the verb 'wake' appears twice (lines 2 and 4) so with 'rouse' there are three references to the act of waking. Why do you think Owen gives emphasis to this activity? There is a brief commentary for you to consult at the end of this section (Commentary A) but discuss the point fully with others first and then write a short sentence which gives an account of your response to the word.

Line 7 It is normal for words to be put in these gaps which are attributes of or which modify our view of the sun. The *early morning* sun, for example, would make a very sound choice and would repeat one other word which has occurred earlier. Another possible choice might be *bright early*. Again this is grammatically correct and suggests a certain optimism, too, that the 'he' could be roused. What were your choices and what were your reasons for selecting them? In fact, Owen wrote:

> 'The *kind old* sun will know'

Is this a strong sun? Do you find this surprising? Does 'sun' now have the same associations as those of the 'sun' in the first few lines? Have you noticed how the sun is personified, that is, described as if it were a person? What other words in stanza 1 are used which give the sun human qualities?

★★★★★

'Gently', 'touch', 'whisper', 'kind', 'old', 'know' are all words which could be applied to a person. Yet Owen writes:

> 'Gently *its* touch awoke him once' (l. 2)
> 'Always *it* woke him' (l. 4)

when it is equally open to him to use the animate personal pronoun. In fact, to put 'he' and 'his' would complete the personification of the sun begun with words like 'touch' and 'whisper'. This is an interesting stylistic point. What are its implications? Discuss this with another student or with others in your group and then consult Commentary B on this point.

Lines 8–14: Discussion

We shall begin discussion of this stanza by considering a word which has not been blanked out. The first word of this stanza is 'think'. What does the word have in common grammatically with the first word of the first stanza? What is different about it? What is the reader being asked to do in this stanza which makes our view of the (now presumably) dead soldier different?

Line 9 In line 9 what word did you choose? Owen wrote:

> '*Woke*, once, the clays of a cold star'

Refer back to your discussion of line 6 and to Commentary A. Notice, too, the verb in line 8. Consider now some other words in lines 8–9. What associations or effects are produced by 'seeds'? Which line in the first stanza does this word recall? What happens when seeds are sown? Why is there reference to *seeds*, *sun* and *waking* in a poem about the futile death of a soldier? Finally, give some thought to the use of the word 'cold'. With which words in the poem does it contrast and with which words does it link in meaning?

Lines 10–11   Try reading these lines aloud. It is very difficult for anyone to read them smoothly or evenly. What are they about? Why are we forced to read them unevenly? What emotions are conveyed directly by our reading? What was your prediction of the word omitted at the end of line 11? If you chose 'move' it is grammatically correct. But was your choice affected by the pattern of words used at the end of each line in this stanza? Owen's choice was:

> 'Are limbs, so dear-achieved, are sides,
> Full-nerved—still warm—too hard to *stir*?'

How would you describe the pattern of end 'rhymes'?

> seeds/sides   star/stir   tall/toil/all

This is another important stylistic feature of the poet's use of language. What are its effects? Discuss this point with others in your group. Note down your conclusions. What would be the effect on you if there were full and complete rhymes in this poem? There is further discussion of this point in Commentary C. Compare your own conclusions with those in the commentary but it may be best to do so after discussion of the gap-filling exercise is finished.

Line 12   The most typical predictions here would probably form a set of words referring to the dead soldier or to natural growth. For example:

> youth   grass   soldier

They could each be justified both grammatically and in relation to other words in the poem. What was your choice? Why did you choose it?
In fact, Owen wrote:

> 'Was it for this the *clay* grew tall?'

Are you surprised by his choice? To what line does this word point back? Why? (It should be noted here that clay can mean both a kind of soil and the substance of the human body.)

Lines 13–14   Again there is a clue here. The space in line 13 is to be filled with a word beginning with 'f'. If you had to choose between:

> O what made *futile* sunbeams toil

and

> O what made *fatuous* sunbeams toil

which would you choose and why? 'Futile' would be a good choice because it makes a pattern with the title of the poem. However, Owen selected *fatuous*. It is similar in meaning to 'futile' but it sounds a little more contemptuous. What are the differences in sound? Does how the word is said affect our attitude to the tone of the final question here? Finally, consider a word in line 14 which you were not asked to predict:

> 'To break earth's *sleep* at all'

It is a word which contrasts with one main pattern of words across the poem. This pattern is grouped around the repetition of the word .... (?) Fill in the gaps in the table below with the other semantic contrasts you can find in the poem. Contrast, too, the associations carried by particular words.

sun	snow
warm	cold
wake	
	....
	death
....	hard
....	
young	....
animacy	inanimacy (it)
growth	....
clay (body)	clay (earth)

SUMMARY

This has not been an exercise where we can start with discussion of the feelings aroused in you by the poem. This is, of course, a pity because it is a very deeply moving poem written out of a profound anguish. The soldier is nameless and we do not even know if he is known to the poet. But the situation is universal. The dead soldier stands for every individual killed in war.

The point of your work in this section has been to help you to recognise some of the ways in which vocabulary can work in a poem. Many of the words here are simple, monosyllabic, almost everyday words; but they produce complex effects both in the way in which they refer to things and the stylistic patterns they make with other words.

Re-read the whole poem (see *Appendix 7*). Then go on to consult the commentaries. If you do not agree with some points in the commentary or have other points which you would prefer to emphasise then write a short paragraph explaining your own ideas about the poem. But, as in these commentaries, make sure that these ideas can be checked by others. To do this, you will need to refer closely to Owen's use of language.

Commentary A

The many references to 'waking' in the poem are poignantly ironic. Just as we know that it will do no good to move the soldier, so we realise that he cannot be woken. He is in a sleep of death. It is a death which ends a short life in a world which comes to seem increasingly futile. Perhaps the sun should never have woken this world in the first place, then these agonies and futilities would not have to be suffered. As we have seen from our work on lines 13 and 14, the poem is structured on numerous contrasts. These contrasts seem to cancel each other out and produce a feeling of emptiness and nothingness. Most prominent among these contrasts is that of waking and sleeping.

Commentary B

Here we may begin by noticing that 'sun', an inanimate noun in the code, has been given the attributes of animacy in the context, and more particularly of humaneness. Thus it is represented as touching the living sleeper to wake him up and as whispering in his ear. Further, its occurrence in the environment 'The kind old . . . will know' suggests that it is to be equated with 'man' or 'woman' which would be normal collocates here. But we must notice that although the context confers human qualities on the sun, at the same time the word retains the quality of inanimacy which accompanies it from the code. The pronouns, we note, are inanimate. So we have here an example of a hybrid unit created by the overlap of extra-textual relations which link the word with the code and intra-textual relations which link the word with other items of language in the context. The sun here is both inanimate and human, and yet, of course, at the same time, neither.

H. G. Widdowson: 'Stylistics' in *Techniques in Applied Linguistics*

Commentary C

Notice the very characteristic use of assonance – sun/sown; once/France; snow/now/know; seeds/sides; star/stir; tall/toil/all. These half-rhymes leave a sense of incompleteness on the ear. Cheated of our natural expectation of a rhyme, we are referred back from the poem itself as a formal triumph (which it is) to the poem's theme: to the frustration of form, of pattern, in the ruthless destructiveness of war.

C. B. Cox and A. E. Dyson: *Modern Poetry: Studies in Practical Criticism*

EXPLOITATION

For further practice fill in the gaps in the following poem by the American poet Emily Dickinson (1830–86). Discuss your choices with others before consulting the complete version of the poem which is printed in *Appendix 8*.

> There's been a Death, in the Opposite House,
>   As lately as Today –
> I know it, by the .... look
>   Such Houses have – alway –
>
> The Neighbors rustle in and out –   5
>   The Doctor – drives away –
> A Window opens like a .... –
>   Abrupt – mechanically –

>>>→

Somebody flings a Mattress out —
  The Children hurry by —   10
They wonder if it died — on that —
  I used to — when a Boy —

The Minister — goes .... in —
  As if the House were His —
And He owned all the Mourners — now — 15
  And little Boys — besides —

And then the Milliner — and the Man
  Of the .... Trade —
To take the measure of the House —
  There'll be that Dark Parade —   20

Of Tassels — and of Coaches — soon —
  It's easy as a Sign —
The Intuition of the News —
  In just a Country Town —

Emily Dickinson

As a final exercise select your own words for blanking out from the following poem. Make sure that you can justify why you would want others to try to predict the words you have omitted. Before attempting this, you may like to re-read your work on this poem in Unit 5, *Language patterns III* and Unit 6, *Vocabulary I*.

*

THE EAGLE

Fragment

He clasps the crag with crooked hands;
Close to the sun in lonely lands,
Ring'd with the azure world, he stands.

The wrinkled sea beneath him crawls;
He watches from his mountain walls,   5
And like a thunderbolt he falls.

Alfred Lord Tennyson

* The recording is to be found within Unit 6.

SECTION B

Orientation: Scrambled stanzas

1 In Section A, *Stylistic analysis* and in Units 5 and 6 we explored the part which word and sentence structures play in style. In this section we will examine how larger units of a literary text combine.

2 The following poem about a snake is by the American poet Emily Dickinson (see also p. 185). Before you begin work on it you should explore your own reactions to snakes. What feelings do you have when you see a snake? Where do you usually see them? How do they move? What kind of creatures are they? Why are some people frightened of them? Use the picture of the snake below. Write a few sentences which describe how you feel. (You may like to re-read D. H. Lawrence's poem 'Snake' on p. 50 first.)

A
The Grass divides as with a Comb —
A spotted shaft is seen —
And then it closes at your feet
And opens further on —

D
He likes a Boggy Acre
A Floor too cool for Corn —
Yet when a Boy, and Barefoot —
I more than once at Noon

B
But never met this Fellow
Attended, or alone
Without a tighter breathing
And Zero at the Bone —

E
Have passed, I thought, a Whip lash
Unbraiding in the Sun
When stooping to secure it
It wrinkled, and was gone —

C
Several of Nature's People
I know, and they know me —
I feel for them a transport
Of cordiality —

F
A narrow Fellow in the Grass
Occasionally rides —
You may have met Him — did you not
His notice sudden is —

3 Now look up the following words:
   transport (the word has more than one meaning)
   cordiality
   braid, braiding
   zero

4 Next re-arrange the stanzas A–F in what you consider to be the appropriate order. Work in groups of three or four. Discuss the reasons for your choice. Can you defend your reasons? Write down the letters which indicate your sequence. Are they the same as those of other groups?
     The sequence in which these stanzas occur in Emily Dickinson's poem is:
           F   B   C   A   D   E   (See the complete text in *Appendix 9*.)
   What are the grammatical reasons for A to follow C?
   Why is F the first stanza?
   Would it be possible to start the poem with B?
   Which of the stanzas is the most general and which is the most specific?
   Which stanza has the most impact?
   Why do you think stanza C runs on into stanza A? These stanzas also contain
     several different clauses which make up the longest sentence in the poem.
   What is the link between (a) the subject matter, and (b) the shape and form of
     these stanzas?
   What words are repeated in the first and last stanzas of the poem?
   What kind of attitude to the snake is suggested by the word
     'Fellow'?
   What do you think is meant by a 'transport of cordiality'?
   What do you understand by 'Zero at the Bone'?
   Why is this the last line of the poem?

5 It would be interesting to compare Emily Dickinson's poem with D. H. Lawrence's 'Snake' (Unit 3). Write a brief comparison of the two poems. Pay particular attention to the feelings aroused by the snakes. Which poem do you prefer?

Stylistic analysis II

In previous units we have examined the language of some literary texts by looking separately at vocabulary, grammar, sound patterns and text. In this section we shall be examining these levels in the organisation of language as they occur together.
     We shall examine a poem by Thomas Hardy, 'The Oxen', with reference to the way in which different kinds of language organisation combine to produce meanings. We shall focus on Hardy's vocabulary, the sounds produced by some of his choices of vocabulary and on the grammar he uses. We shall attempt to describe the style of the poem. Here is the poem:

118

The Oxen

CHRISTMAS EVE, and twelve of the clock.
   'Now they are all on their knees,'
An elder said as we sat in a flock
   By the embers in hearthside ease.

We pictured the meek mild creatures where   5
   They dwelt in their strawy pen,
Nor did it occur to one of us there
   To doubt they were kneeling then.

So fair a fancy few would weave
   In these years! Yet, I feel,
If someone said on Christmas Eve,   10
   'Come; see the oxen kneel

'In the lonely barton by yonder coomb
   Our childhood used to know,'
I should go with him in the gloom,   15
   Hoping it might be so.

Thomas Hardy

The poem is set on Christmas Eve, the day before Jesus Christ was born. The poem hints at a belief that God is so powerful that animals would be moved to kneel as they sensed the birth of God's son, Jesus, and as the birth was celebrated each year thereafter.

1 Before we start work on the poem's language, it might be useful to think back to your own childhood. Did you have experiences as a child which you would now dismiss? Did anything happen to you which you believed in at the time but now no longer believe in? If so, write two short paragraphs, one describing the experience, the other describing your present view of it. Re-read the poem.

2 Try reading the poem aloud. Using the scales from Unit 4 *Orientation* describe in a few words how you would read it (fast–slow, loud–soft etc.). Discuss this with another student. Then listen to the cassette. Now write a few sentences which summarise what you think the poem is about. You are not on this occasion asked to summarise what happens but to say why the writer wants to describe to us what happened.

   Once again the use of stars (*****) means that the question is a more difficult one and requires extra thought. Where you see the key symbol (🗝) and a number (i–vi) we have supplied suggested answers and guidelines for you at the end of the unit.

⟫→

Grammar

3 Begin by following the patterns of tense in the poem. What is the dominant tense in the first two stanzas? Write out the verbs which fit this category.

🗝 (i)   ★★★★★

Can a pattern easily be seen in the next two stanzas? If so, what is it?

★★★★★

There are only two sentences and one is very much longer than the other. Find the main verb in this second sentence from 'Yet I feel,' (line 10) to the end of the poem.

🗝 (ii)   ★★★★★

Is it connected with other verbs in the same tense?
   The verb pattern is much more complicated in these last two stanzas. There is a link with the present participle (hoping) in line 16, but the predominant pattern is one of different kinds of *modal* verbs. For example:
   'So fair a fancy few *would* weave' (l. 9)
   'Our childhood *used* to know, (l. 14)
   I *should* go with him in the gloom, (l. 15)
   Hoping it *might* be so.' (l. 16)
There are also imperatives, line 12 'Come; see . . .' and a simple past, line 11 'said'.

4 If you wrote an account according to instructions in number 1, how does your use of tense differ from Hardy's in 'The Oxen'? You probably have one stanza written in the past tense and another written in the present. Why is there no such simple contrast in the poem? There is clearly an opposition between how things are now and how they were. So, why does the poet not reflect this simple opposition in his use of verbs? This question should be discussed in pairs or with other members of your class. On this occasion you may use either English or your own native language.

5 Stanzas 3 and 4 are certainly more difficult to read and understand. The tense pattern, the type of verbs used and the clause pattern are very varied and complex. It is in marked contrast to the language, style and content of the opening two stanzas. Notice also the differences in *personal pronouns*. In the first two stanzas 'we' is used. In the second two stanzas what is the pronoun used? What are the reasons for this?

6 It is necessary now to explore why Hardy has chosen to make this contrast between the clauses.
   What is the subject matter covered in stanzas 1 and 2?
   How does it contrast with the subject matter of stanzas 3 and 4?
   Discuss this with members of your group. Is there a change in attitude in stanzas 3 and 4?

Do you think it is a simple matter that the adult of the present time is no longer able to accept the word of the child? This is an important feature of the poem. It is marked in the style of the poem.

Give these questions some thought, paying particular attention to the meanings carried by the final line of the poem (line 16):

'Hoping it might be so'

Vocabulary

Examining the poem's grammar takes us quite a long way. But other patterns contribute other layers of meaning. Vocabulary is especially significant.

7 *Stanzas 1 and 2*
Look up some of the following words in a dictionary:
a) flock
b) meek and mild
c) elder
d) embers
What associations are produced for you by the words together?

🔑─⊰ (iii)   ★★★★★

8 *Stanzas 3 and 4*
The most striking words here are 'barton' and 'coomb'. You may not find them in your dictionary. They are dialect words. More specifically they are words used in the dialects of S. W. England, the region with which Thomas Hardy was most intimately connected.

It almost doesn't matter if you don't know the precise meaning of these words. It is not necessary to know the meaning of every single word in a poem in order to be able to appreciate it. Here it is almost enough for the poet to evoke distant times in the past (the word 'yonder' is an archaism meaning 'over there') and to suggest the settled village community in which such words might be used.

Another key word here is 'gloom'. Explore the meaning of this word by setting it alongside related words and working out its specific connotations.

Put a tick or question mark in the appropriate box of the chart below. 'Dusk' has been completed for you.

	no light	little light	uncertainty	unhappy mood	feeling of pessimism
gloom					
dark					
dusk		✓	✓		
mystery					

The vocabulary in this poem is especially suggestive. In Wilfred Owen's 'Futility' simple and direct words were often used for the purposes of ironic contrast. Here the use of vocabulary is a little more *symbolic*.

What is the word from the first stanza with which 'gloom' can be linked?

🗝 (iv) ★★★★★

'Gloom' suggests a certain degree of pessimism – as we can see, for example, from the sentence:

He is very gloomy about the prospects for the British economy. (despondent, pessimistic)

though we should remember here that the word is followed by the final line of the poem – '*Hoping* it *might* be so' – which to some extent counteracts the feelings produced by 'gloom'. In the light of your work on the poem's vocabulary return now to question 2 and modify your sentences on the poem, if you think it is necessary.

Sound and the Poem

9 Is there a line in the poem where the sound strikes you particularly?

★★★★★

For us line 9 is particularly striking. Certain sounds are prominent. 'f' and 'w' sounds are put closely together. Why?

'So fair a fancy few would weave
In these years!'

🗝 (v) ★★★★★

In many ways this is quite a pivotal line between stanzas 1 and 2 and the long complicated clause pattern of stanzas 3 and 4. It stands between two worlds. The world of the past 'then' and the world of 'these years', the world of community 'we' and the world of isolation 'I'. It might also concentrate our attention on the fair fancy which few would weave; that is, few these days would believe or imagine that oxen kneel on Christmas Eve. The sounds appear a little scornful or dismissive of such superstition (note the light explosion of air in 'f' and 'w'). However, it is perhaps not quite so simple as this. The next word is 'yet'. We are prepared for the speaker to explore an alternative viewpoint.

10 Now look back at the discussion of rhyme in Wilfred Owen's 'Futility' (p. 113). What is the rhyme pattern in 'The Oxen'? Does it surprise you?

★★★★★

In reading literature we should try to make links between both the words and the poetic forms used by the poet and the meanings and feelings the writer wants to express and evoke in us. What links would you make in this poem?

🗝 (vi) ★★★★★

Finally, return to number 2 above and re-read the poem aloud in the light of the above discussion and analysis. Again, discuss your reading.

EXPLOITATION

Look back at the poem. Consider particularly the speaker's perspective. What stylistic features create this perspective?
Now read this commentary. How does it compare with your analysis of the poem?

Commentary on 'The Oxen'

The speaker, however, is not an 'elder' but a member of the sceptical modern world who looks back towards a disappearing age. Rationalism has replaced religious faith, *yet* not entirely. Hardy holds knowing and unknowing, disbelief and belief, in suspension. The poem would be unbalanced if Hardy had subtracted either the possibility for belief or the necessity of disbelief. Its poignance lies in the crucial division of awareness, its delicate rendering of mingled hope and nostalgia.

Adapted from Paul Zietlow: *Moments of Vision: The Poetry of Thomas Hardy*

SUMMARY OF THE UNIT

1 Different texts will, of course, have different stylistic features. In this unit we have learned that the following features can be important:
   a) Choices in vocabulary.
   b) Links between words (including contrasts and symbolic associations).
   c) The overlap of words and sound patterns (including rhyme).
   d) Tense.
   e) Clause structure (especially simple versus complex).
   f) Personal pronouns.
   g) Types and mood of the verb (e.g. imperative/interrogative, modal etc.).
   h) Sentence linkage (conjunctions etc.).
2 This is the most linguistic or linguistic–stylistic unit of this book. Analysing the style of a poem or short story or extract from a novel is difficult. Writers can produce very interesting but complex effects with words. We can become deeply moved and involved in what they write. It is often the case that deeply moving responses are awoken in us by complex uses of language even though on the surface the language may appear simple. It it the task of stylistic analysis to help us to explain how language is used to produce these responses and effects.
3 Stylistic analysis works by putting texts under a microscope. But there is always a danger of losing sight of the whole. That is why it is very important to keep reading and discussing the texts that are put under the microscope and to ask yourself what the ideas, emotions and themes they depict mean to you.
   Remember, though, that our stylistic units are designed to show that what is said is very closely bound up with how it is written.

4 Unit 7 examined the style of different types of English, including literary texts. You will be able to extend what you have learned in this unit when you have re-read Unit 7. Unit 10, in contrast with this unit, deals with a long narrative. It is clearly very difficult to examine the contribution of every word, clause or sentence with such a long text. The approach to stylistic analysis introduced in Units 7 and 8 work best with shorter texts.

SUGGESTED ANSWERS AND GUIDELINES

🗝 (i) 'Said', 'pictured', 'sat', 'dwelt' are all in the simple past tense. 'Did it occur' has its auxiliary verb in the simple past tense too. 'Were kneeling' is past continuous.

🗝 (ii) The main verb is 'feel'. It is in the present tense.

🗝 (iii) The word 'flock' suggests a tightly knit community. People are like a 'flock' of sheep following one another closely and unquestioningly. 'Meek' and 'mild' are, as you may have discovered, words which are often used in Christian prayers and hymns to refer to Jesus Christ. An 'elder' is another 'religious' word used to denote the leading member of a village community. It is interesting to ask at this point what the significance of 'embers' might be. The people are clearly sitting around a fire. They are comfortable and at ease. But the fire is dying. Only a few embers remain. Could there be any symbolic meaning to this?

🗝 (iv) 'Gloom' links with 'embers' to suggest that it is still difficult to *see* clearly – especially what is 'true' and what is merely weaving a 'fancy'. It evokes uncertainty. Dark times are upon us and things are not as they were. The embers of an older community or way of life provide even less light now than 'then' (line 8).

🗝 (v) The concentration of these sounds seems to draw attention to what is being said. These lines are an example of alliteration. Alliteration describes a repetition of the same consonants (here 'f' and 'w').

🗝 (vi) Here perhaps Hardy feels a pattern of belief is still possible. The loss of a previous way of life and belief is not total. A framework exists and that is reflected in regular and full rhyme pattern.

Unit 9 'The Moving Finger writes': Background

Introduction for the student

In this unit we explore the backgrounds to some literary texts. We have stressed how important it is to examine carefully the 'web of words' from which texts are made, as we believe this provides a basis for understanding, appreciation and interpretation. The words we find on the page, however, are not everything. Knowledge of the life of the author, or the times in which he or she lived, or of influential ideas current at the time of writing a particular work, can also help us.

   Although this unit supplies some information, its main aim is to help you to decide what kind of background information may be necessary and how to find out about it.

Orientation

1 Read the text on the left without reference to the notes on the right. You will almost certainly find that though you may understand the sentences you do not know at first 'what it is about'. This is because you do not have the necessary background information, which the newspaper assumes in a majority of its readers. This information is incorporated in summary form, from paragraph four on.

Re-read the text in conjunction with the notes provided.

'Dingo' appeal rejected

By Denis Warner in Melbourne

Three Federal Court judges in Sydney yesterday dismissed Mrs. Lindy Chamberlain's appeal against her conviction in the 'dingo baby' case.
5   They ordered 35-year-old Mrs. Chamberlain to be delivered to the Berrinah Jail in Darwin as soon as convenient to resume her sentence of life imprisonment with hard labour
10 for the murder of her infant daughter

Problems and solutions of the background

What is a dingo? Why inverted commas? The reader assumes it is an appeal against conviction in a court. But conviction for what?

   The place names indicate that the case and presumably the crime took place in Australia. But what is the 'dingo baby' case?

⟫→

125

Azaria at Ayers Rock in Central
Australia.

As soon as the appeal was dismissed, Mrs. Chamberlain's lawyers
15 applied for a stay of the imprisonment
order, but this was refused. The lawyers later sought leave to appeal to the
High Court which may hear her application for renewed bail on Monday.

20 The case began with the disappearance of Azaria from a tent in a holiday
park near Ayers Rock in August,
1980. Mrs. Chamberlain maintained
that the baby had been taken by a
25 dingo (Australian wild dog).

Background begins.

New baby

We are told what a 'dingo' is, and what
happened. We can now explain the
inverted commas in the heading.

After two inquests, she was found
guilty of murder, at a trial in Darwin
but was released on bail after the birth
three weeks later of her fourth child,
30 Kablia.

Mrs. Chamberlain maintained her
composure throughout yesterday's
brief court session. Her husband
Michael, a 38-year-old Seventh Day
35 Adventist minister also appeared
calm after hearing the court dismiss
his appeal against his conviction for
disposing of nine-week-old Azaria's
body.

40 The husband, under a suspended
sentence as an accessory after the fact,
left court with Kablia and church
officials for his living quarters at an
Adventist college.

45 At the Darwin trial, the jury unani-
mously decided Mrs. Chamberlain slit
her daughter's throat in the family car
at Ayers Rock. But the prosecution
never found the body or a murder
50 weapon.

Further background information is
provided.

The Daily Telegraph

2 Work in pairs. Retell the story to your partner 'from the beginning'. One
possible opening might be 'Sometime in August 1980 this family, the
Chamberlains, were camping near Ayers Rock . . .' The person listening should
note how the word 'dingo' is first introduced, and how many times the word is
used. Then reverse roles.

3 Find a similar example from an English language newspaper, and make a note of
(a) the new information and (b) the background. In the example in number 1 it is
not possible to answer the question 'What is the "dingo baby" case?' without the
background. Make two questions of this type for the article you have selected.

4 In the 'late news' or 'stop press' section of a newspaper, background information

is omitted. Find an example, again from an English language newspaper, and indicate what background is necessary to 'complete the picture'.

5 In literary text it is unusual for the background to be given in the concentrated form of an on-going newspaper report, though it is possible to find examples. Here is such an example:

> Mr Caldwell was born 21 December 1896, on Staten Island, New York City. His father was the Reverend John Wesley Caldwell, a graduate of Princeton University and the Union Theological Seminary, New York. Upon graduation from the latter place he entered the Presbyterian ministry, making his the fifth genera- 5
> tion of clergymen supplied by the Caldwell family to this denomination. His wife, née Phyllis Harthorne, was of Southern extraction, hailing from the near environs of Nashville, Tennessee.

John Updike: *The Centaur*

Though this example is similar to a newspaper in information content it has some noticeable differences in style and choice of words. Underline any words or phrases which you think are unlikely to occur in newspaper 'background'.

When background is provided in this way it is most likely to occur at the beginning, or in the first two or three pages of a story. It is almost impossible to provide it in this way in poetry or drama. Use your library facilities to find one further example of a concentrated background to a short story or novel.

Novels, by their extent alone, frequently do provide the background, though in a fragmented way which requires the reader to fit the pieces together, like a jig-saw puzzle. In other cases the characters, either by speech or action, or the comments of others, give clues to social, geographical or temperamental circumstances which the writer is trying to convey. There are nevertheless some obvious areas in English literature where we would like more background than is provided by the author. However much he or she has already provided, it would still be helpful to have the background in 'concentrated' form. Such areas might include:

a) the Victorian Age, for the novels of Dickens;

b) 'Wessex', for the novels of Hardy;

c) early 20th century working-class conditions, for some of the novels of D. H. Lawrence.

There are, of course, many other such areas.

Background I

1 Read the following extract from 'The Force of Circumstance' by W. Somerset Maugham. The complete story occurs in Unit 10.

> It was hard to realize that nine months ago she had never even heard of him. She had met him at a small place by the seaside where she was spending a month's holiday with her mother. Doris was a secretary to a member of parliament, Guy was home on leave. They were staying at the same hotel, and he quickly told 5 her all about himself. He was born in Sembulu, where his father had served for thirty years under the second Sultan, and on leaving school he had entered the same service. He was devoted to the country.
> 'After all, England's a foreign land to me,' he told her. 'My 10 home's Sembulu.'
> And now it was her home too. He asked her to marry him at the end of the month's holiday. She had known he was going to, and had decided to refuse him. She was her widowed mother's only child and she could not go so far away from her, but when the 15 moment came she did not quite know what happened to her, she was carried off her feet by an unexpected emotion, and she accepted him. They had been settled now for four months in the little outstation of which he was in charge. She was very happy.

Somerset Maugham: *The Force of Circumstance*

Consider the implications of the word 'outstation'. What is the background to an 'outstation'? Why is it there? Who lives there? What is Guy's position in the 'outstation'?

Answer these questions from your own knowledge of the world, then, when you have read the complete story in Unit 10, provide further evidence.

2 Imagine that you are making a film of 'The Force of Circumstance' (see Unit 2). The opening is to be a two-minute 'shot' of the outstation. Describe it. What buildings are there? How big are they? What are the roads like? What form of transportation can be seen?

Background II

This book includes two poems or extracts from the work of Thomas Hardy (see pp. 119 and 130). The poem which follows 'When I Set Out For Lyonnesse' is a personal record of Hardy's life, and without 'background' much of the intensity of the poem is lost. The 'magic in my eyes' of the last stanza is little different from the lyrics of a modern pop song, without some awareness of Hardy's life. This is given in the background notes below. The task will be to relate the biographical material to the details of the poem.

128

1 Read the following notes.

Thomas Hardy was professionally an architect, for which he trained as a young man. In the 1860s, in his twenties, Hardy lived in London, following his profession, while reading widely and writing in his spare time. He was not yet an established writer, and the prospect of earning enough money to live entirely from his writing seemed remote. Meanwhile Hardy made steady if unspectacular progress in his profession, with a specialisation in restoring old churches, and in 1870 he was working with a small office in Weymouth, on the south coast of England, not far from his birthplace. Up to this time Hardy seems to have had only limited contact with women, though he admired and wrote to a cousin called Tryphena Sparks. At the personal level Hardy was a somewhat shy and lonely man. His professional background, and his time in London, did not disguise the fact that he was at heart a countryman, with a deep and life-long sympathy for his native 'Wessex'*. He was conscious of the difficulties of the true countryman in adapting to professional city life, and he wrote about this conflict in several novels, in particular in the character of Clym Yeobright in his novel *The Return of the Native* (published 1878).

In 1870 Thomas Hardy himself fell in love. The occasion was, by chance, connected with his professional life as an architect. He was required by his office to go and look at an old church in the extreme west of England, in the county of Cornwall, which even today, with modern communications, is relatively remote. The details are recorded here in a modern biography.

It concerned the mouldering parish church of St Juliot, near Boscastle, in North Cornwall, with its dropsical and dangerous tower, needing a massive restoration long-delayed by lack of money and an absentee patron who lived in Antigua. Hicks surveyed it and drew up a plan in April 1867; but only two   5
months later, the wife of the elderly rector, the Reverend Caddell Holder, died, and the plan was put into cold storage. However, the rector quickly married again, this time a woman half his age, who, like Hicks, came from a Bristol family, and she took up the cause of church restoration with energy. Then Hicks himself   10
died, but his successor was pursued with summonses to St Juliot, and wrote to Hardy on 11 February, asking him to go and make a fresh survey at this remote place, all expenses paid. Hardy, intent on getting the novel off to Macmillan, did not at once respond; but after another urgent appeal from Crickmay, he   15
set off at four o'clock in the starlight from Bockhampton on Monday, 7 March. It took him twelve hours by various trains to reach Launceston, from which he had to hire a trap to go the final sixteen or seventeen miles. A poem he drafted shortly afterwards describes his thoughts of Tryphena Sparks in her college in   20

* 'Wessex' is the fictional name given by Hardy to the southern part of England comprising largely the counties of Dorset, Wiltshire and parts of Hampshire.

London as he progressed toward a spot that seemed as far west from her as it could possibly be. Indeed, he was scribbling a poem on a piece of blue paper now. As the fine day darkened in the early March evening, his journey took on a weird strangeness, heightened by the approaching sound of the Atlantic breakers, and the swivelling flash of the coastal lighthouses. A small lane to the left led to the rectory, and he rang the bell in complete darkness, hastily thrusting the blue paper with the poem into his pocket. He was led into the drawing-room, and found there neither the rector, who had suddenly retired to bed with gout, nor his wife, who was nursing him. Instead, he was received by a young lady in a brown dress. She was a full-bosomed creature with a high colour, bright blue eyes and masses of blonde hair. Her open-air complexion and her energetic movements were dazzling to the tired traveller. In her extreme vitality, she seemed unlike any woman he had met before. She was the rector's sister-in-law, Emma Lavinia Gifford, Hardy's future wife.

Robert Gittings: *Young Thomas Hardy*

2 Read this poem. Then listen to the recording.

 When I Set Out For Lyonnesse
                        (1870)

When I set out for Lyonnesse,
        A hundred miles away,
        The rime was on the spray,
And starlight lit my lonesomeness
        When I set out for Lyonnesse   5
        A hundred miles away.

What would bechance at Lyonnesse
        While I should sojourn there
        No prophet durst declare,
        Nor did the wisest wizard guess   10
What would bechance at Lyonnesse
        While I should sojourn there.

When I came back from Lyonnesse
        With magic in my eyes,
        All marked with mute surmise   15
My radiance rare and fathomless,
When I came back from Lyonnesse
        With magic in my eyes!

Thomas Hardy

3 Work in pairs. Answer these questions by referring first to the poem and then to the corresponding background notes.

   a) 'Lyonnesse' in the poem is a fictitious place name. What is the real place name indicated in the background notes?

   b) Hardy says 'The rime was on the spray' and, in the next line, mentions 'starlight'. What, in a simple sentence, is he telling us about his journey?

   c) 'lonesomeness' in line 4 could indicate that Hardy set out alone. What else could it refer to in Hardy's life at that time?

   d) The second stanza could be summarised as:
       'Nobody could foretell what would happen while I was at "Lyonnesse".'
       Why did Hardy go there, and what in fact did happen?

   e) What is the 'magic' referred to in stanza 3?

   f) Hardy writes of 'my radiance rare and fathomless'. This most probably refers to the person he met. But the notes mention a 'weird strangeness'. What is the possible connection between the two?

EXPLOITATION

This is essentially a happy poem. Find another poem by Hardy (not necessarily autobiographical) where 'love' does not lead to happiness.

131

Background III

1 First listen to, and then read the following stanzas carefully.

    Calm is the morn without a sound,
        Calm as to suit a calmer grief,
        And only through the faded leaf
    The chestnut pattering to the ground:

    Calm and deep peace on this high wold,   5
        And on these dews that drench the furze,
        And all the silvery gossamers
    That twinkle into green and gold:

    Calm and still light on yon great plain
        That sweeps with all its autumn bowers,   10
        And crowded farms and lessening towers,
    To mingle with the bounding main:

    Calm and deep peace in this wide air,
        These leaves that redden to the fall;
        And in my heart, if calm at all,   15
    If any calm, a calm despair:

    Calm on the seas, and silver sleep,
        And waves that sway themselves in rest,
        And dead calm in that noble breast
    Which heaves but with the heaving deep.   20

    Alfred Lord Tennyson

This is part of a very long poem by Tennyson called 'In Memoriam', published in 1850. Each of the stanzas begins with the word 'calm', and that word occurs no less than eleven times in these five stanzas. At a first reading the poet seems to be contemplating the calm of death after life, in a way reminiscent of Spencer's line:
    'Ease after war, death after life does greatly please.'
But a glance at the background to 'In Memoriam', shows this to be very far from true. The information which follows is, in a sense, biographical, but because the poem is the result of a deeply felt event, over which the poet had no control, we prefer to categorise it as 'experiential'. It is of course still 'background' to the text, and without it the full effect of the poem could not be appreciated.

2 Read the following notes before answering the questions in number 3.

Tennyson is usually considered the great poet of the Victorian Age, which covers the period from 1840 to 1900. Tennyson himself was born in 1809 and died in 1892, so his life as a writer and poet corresponds closely with the reign of Queen Victoria. In later life Tennyson became a great social figure, frequently visiting the houses of the rich and famous   5
and reading his own poetry there. This was very different from his life as

a young man. He came from a large family living in rural Lincolnshire, in
eastern England. The family, however, though talented, was afflicted
with illness, and much bitterness and quarrelling, so that Tennyson's
early years were not particularly happy. This changed during his years at   10
Cambridge University, where he became an active member of a group of
young men of similar interests – mostly philosophical and literary – who
called themselves 'The Apostles'. One of the group was a man called
Arthur Hallam, a lively and intelligent person of whom great things were
expected in the future. Tennyson and Hallam became great friends,   15
respected and admired each other's intellect, and greatly enjoyed each
other's company. Hallam provided just the company and stimulus
Tennyson needed to relieve the loneliness he often suffered when he
returned to Lincolnshire.

Tennyson and Hallam made a journey to the Rhine in 1832. On a   20
similar European trip a year later with his father, Hallam died suddenly
in Vienna. His body was brought home later for burial in England (a).

The Victorian period was much concerned, especially in poetry, with death. But there is no doubt that Hallam's death affected Tennyson deeply and personally. Seventeen years later he published a poem called 'In Memoriam A.H.H.', at which he had been working intermittently during the whole of that time. A.H.H. is his friend Arthur Hallam. In fact the whole poem is not about Hallam, but about Tennyson (b) and his reactions to Hallam's death. His admiration for Hallam is, of course, clear in the poem (c). The poem, though very long, has little 'story' – Tennyson had no great skill as a narrative writer – but a great deal of analysis of the poet's feelings (d). 25

30

'In Memoriam' fits only very loosely together, and draws on ideas from theology, immortality and many other areas. Section XI is quoted above. The setting seems to be Tennyson's native Lincolnshire (e). He perceives the calm of autumn (f) as he looks out towards the sea (g). The sea reminds him of the homecoming of Hallam, but there it is not the natural and pleasant calm of autumn, but 'dead calm' – an unnatural calm (h). The reader faces a sudden shock. This is no longer the calm we seek, but the presence of something terrible, at least to someone who has lost a dear friend. 35

40

3 Answer the following questions about the poem, now that you have read the information in the background notes. The letters (a–h) inserted in the notes correspond to the questions.
   a) Paraphrase the last four lines of the poem in such a way as to make clear that the body of Hallam was brought back to England by sea.
   b) Where in the poem does Tennyson refer to himself, and what, apparently, is his mood?
   c) Which words show that Tennyson admired Hallam?
   d) Which single word would you choose in the poem itself to describe the poet's feelings?
   e) Find three places in the poem which could be descriptions of Lincolnshire.
   f) Autumn is actually mentioned, but what other references are there in the poem to the season?
   g) Two phrases are used for the sea (in addition to the word 'seas'). What are they?
   h) What are the two things referred to by 'dead calm'?

EXPLOITATION

'Most people get over grief, Tennyson seems to enjoy it.'
Discuss this statement in groups of five. Take a stand 'for' or 'against' and try and support your view with words from the poem. There is no need to make a speech – argue your view informally.

Background IV

The following poem, 'After the Battle' which was also used in Unit 4 is also
markedly experiential, and refers to the First World War (see also 'The General',
p. 55 and 'Futility', pp. 110–11).

1 Recall the work you did on reading this poem aloud in Unit 4 and the special
   features which it invites in that respect. Read it again silently.

 *

After the Battle

So they are satisfied with our Brigade,
    And it remains to parcel out the bays!
And we shall have the usual Thanks Parade,
    The beaming General, and the soapy praise.

You will come up in your capricious car   5
    To find your heroes sulking in the rain,
To tell us how magnificent we are,
    And how you hope we'll do the same again.

And we, who knew your old abusive tongue,
    Who heard you hector us a week before,   10
We who have bled to boost you up a rung —
    A K.C.B. perhaps, perhaps a Corps —

We who must mourn those spaces in the mess,
    And somehow fill those hollows in the heart,
We do not want your Sermon on Success,   15
    Your greasy benisons on Being Smart.

We only want to take our wounds away.
    To some warm village where the tumult ends,
And drowsing in the sunshine many a day,
    Forget our aches, forget that we had friends.   20

Weary we are of blood and noise and pain;
    This was a week we shall not soon forget;
And if, indeed, we have to fight again,
    We little wish to think about it yet.

We have done well; we like to hear it said   25
    Say it, and then, for God's sake, say no more.
Fight, if you must, fresh battles far ahead,
    But keep them dark behind your chateau door!

A. P. Herbert

* The recording is to be found within Unit 4.

2 Now read these background notes.

Every English town and village has a monument of some kind as a
memorial to the men from that place who were killed in action in the
First and Second World Wars. The lists of names of those killed are
invariably much longer for the First World War.

This does not mean that the Second World War was in some way a   5
'good' war, and the First World War a 'bad' war. What it does mean is
that the First World War was particularly, prodigally, wasteful of
life (a). The names of the big battles of that war, Somme, Ypres, Loos,
Vimy Ridge and many others are known to many people well over 60
years later, who are not in the least interested in war. They suggest death   10
and horror on a scale not previously known.

There have been few attempts to make films of these battles. There is
little glamour attached to them, though there was undoubtedly much
individual courage and bravery (b). A word much used to describe the
type of warfare was 'attrition'. This means that the opposing armies   15
faced one another with little hope of a breakthrough, and only one tactic
– to pound the opposition until they had no resources left. On both sides
thousands died in this exhausting and fruitless process. In 1914,
however, there was widespread public support for the war. Soldiers were
cheered as they left London to go to fight in northern France. There was   20
no shortage of volunteers to go to the battle. It was not until 1916 that an
awareness of the waste, futility and hopelessness of it all began to creep
in (c).

The war has been much written about, and, looked at. From a distance
in time it seems that there are two main reasons for the immense and   25
tragic waste of life. One was a weapon – the machine gun, which both
sides had. A group of men charging forward was certain to be torn apart
by the repeated rapid fire of this weapon, even if they could overcome the
mud and barbed wire which held them up. The second reason was
human: the officers and leaders. Many of these men were elderly, with   30
experience of fierce but mobile and limited wars, in such places as Sudan
and South Africa years before. These officers believed that 'one more
push' would bring victory, which would make their reputation (d).
Nobody questioned their integrity or patriotism, but their judgement
was something else – it was suspect (e), and by 1916 there were many   35
fighting men who realised this, and were disillusioned with the war (f).
An officer might see the loss of a few *thousand* more men as a small price
to pay for victory, but to the survivors it was obvious that their hope of
seeing the end of the war was small. Men were being thrown away in
repeated attacks which constantly failed (g). And, to them, the reason   40
for it all seemed less and less connected with the enemy, who suffered
equally, than with the pride of the leaders (h). As this continued, soldiers
were themselves less concerned with military achievement, and wanted
only to get away from it all (i). But still, right up to the Armistice in
November 1918, the horrors continued (j).   45

⟫⟶

3 Answer the following questions about the poem, now that you have read the information in the background notes. The letters (a–j) inserted in the notes correspond to the questions.
   a) Which line(s) of the poem indicate the terrible waste of life in the war?
   b) Which words suggest the courage and bravery of the soldiers?
   c) There are several words that suggest futility and hopelessness. Which, in your opinion, do so most effectively?
   d) Find evidence in the poem for officers being concerned with their reputation.
   e) Can you find any evidence here that the judgement of the General was faulty?
   f) 'Say it, and then, for God's sake, say no more.' How does this line suggest disillusionment?
   g) Is there any evidence in the poem to suggest *failure*, rather than *success*?
   h) Which line(s) indicate the pride of the leaders in the war?
   i) The poet talks about getting away from the war to 'some warm village?' Why a *village*? Why *warm*?
   j) Find evidence that the war has by no means ended with this battle.

EXPLOITATION

1 The title of this unit, 'The Moving Finger writes' is given without comment. In fact this is a quotation from *The Rubaiyat of Omar Khayyam*, a title which, on first acquaintance, certainly seems to require background information. Do some research to find answers to the following questions:
   a) When was the poem written, and by whom?
   b) Who was Omar Khayyam?
   c) The translator links the separate stanzas of *Omar Khayyam* together, with a consistent theme. What is that theme? Is it joyful or sad?
   This is the stanza from which the title was taken:

> The Moving Finger writes, and, having writ,
> Moves on; nor all your Piety nor Wit
>   Shall lure it back to cancel half a Line,
> Nor all your Tears wash out a Word of it.
>   (stanza 71)

2 Answer questions (d), (e) and (f) as a preface to the more open-ended question (g).
   d) What does the 'Moving Finger' refer to?
   e) Is there anything in either the language, the thought or the style to suggest an 'old' or medieval poem?
   f) Look back to the poem 'Ozymandias' (Unit 3 *Orientation*). How does the main idea of this stanza compare with the theme of 'Ozymandias'?
   g) Suggest reasons (several) why the opening four words have been used as the title of this unit.

Background V

In the texts in II, III and IV above, the 'background' constituted an additional unit of information, rounding out and perhaps increasing the impact of the text itself. But it is also possible for background to be the core of the whole; in other words, the psychological, religious, or political environment which caused the work to be written in the first place. The reader is likely to have some knowledge of the background, but much of it will probably still be unfamiliar. It is therefore important for you to ask the right sort of questions as you read.

In this text there is no ambiguity about the force or influence which has caused the work to be written. It is openly, unashamedly, political. However it does not seek either to explain or justify a political system, but to reveal its effects rather than the system itself.

1 Read the following extract.

> Spies – there were up to five spies in every gang, but they were
> not necessarily the real thing. Their records showed them as
> spies, but they had probably been simply prisoners-of-war.
> Shukhov was that kind of spy.
> But the Moldavian – he had been the real thing. 5
> The Chief Escort Guard looked down at his list, and his face
> blackened. If a real spy had indeed got away – then the Chief
> Escort Guard would be for it.
> In the crowd, everybody, including Shukhov, went mad. Who
> did he think he was, this vulture, this swine, bastard, shit, 10
> fucker? The sky was already dark, and what light there was came
> from the moon. The stars were out, and the night frost was
> gathering strength – and now this Moldavian bastard was
> missing! Hadn't the shit worked enough that day? Weren't the
> regulation hours – eleven hours from dawn to dusk – sufficiently 15
> long for him? Well, maybe the public prosecutor would add to
> them!
> It was extraordinary to Shukhov that anyone could work so
> hard as not to notice the signal to knock off.
> Shukhov had completely forgotten that he himself had been 20
> working like that only recently – that he had been irritated that
> everybody else had collected around the guard-room excessively
> early. Now he was frozen stiff like the rest of them, furious like
> the rest of them, and it seemed to him that if the Moldavian kept
> them hanging around for another half hour, and if the escort 25
> guards gave him to the crowd – then they'd tear him to pieces,
> like wolves would a lamb!
> The cold was really biting into them now! Nobody stood still –
> either they stamped their feet up and down where they stood, or
> walked two or three paces backwards and forwards. 30

People were discussing whether the Moldavian could have escaped. Well, if he had got away during the day, that was one thing, but if he had hidden and was waiting for the escort guards to leave their watch-towers, he'd have a long time to wait. If there were no traces under the wire to indicate his point of escape – they'd scour the site for three days, and leave the escort guards in the watch-towers for three days, until they found him. Or a week, if necessary. That was as it was laid down, as all the old prisoners knew. In general, if somebody got away, the guards' lives were made hell, and they were kept at it without sleep or food. Sometimes, they got so mad that the escaper wouldn't be brought back alive.

Alexander Solzhenitsyn (translated by Gillon Aitken): *One Day in the Life of Ivan Denisovich*

2 In groups prepare a talk on the background to the text above. The following questions may help you, but you do not have to restrict yourselves to these. Write your background in note form.
   a) What do you know about the author?
       (Use library facilities if necessary.)
   b) Who is the narrator?
   c) Where does it take place?
   d) Why are they there?
   e) Is this direct experience, or a fictional account, or a mixture of both? Can you find any evidence in the text for your decision?
   f) Is there any predominant emotion in this text – for example, anger, misery, hatred, bitterness, determination etc.?
       (Find features in the language which support your choice.)
   g) Who are the prisoners? Who are the guards?
       More important, why are they prisoners?
       This should give you the direction for (h).
   h) What is the political system underlying the story?

3 Choose one person from each group to give the talk to another group. Then discuss any differences in your findings.

EXPLOITATION: RESEARCH READING

Two other books which have similar backgrounds are *Nineteen Eighty-Four* by George Orwell and *Darkness at Noon* by Arthur Koestler. Try and find out as much as you can about the above books. What are the differences in background between these books and *Ivan Denisovich*? Which seems to be the most severe indictment of a system?

Background VI

1 Another 'idea' behind a great deal of modern literature is psychology, and, particularly, the writings of Sigmund Freud (1856–1939). As in the text in *Background V* with a political background, it often becomes difficult to isolate distinct features of background, which take over and pervade the whole. It is necessary to know, however, how Freudian psychology and literature interact. The quotation which follows is not from a literary text, but a book about literature.

Watching his grandson playing in his pram one day, Freud observed him throwing a toy out of the pram and exclaiming *fort!* (gone away), then hauling it in again on a string to the cry of *da!* (here). This, the famous *fort-da* game, Freud interpreted in *Beyond the Pleasure Principle* (1920) as the infant's symbolic mastery of its mother's absence; but it can also   5 be read as the first glimmerings of narrative. *Fort-da* is perhaps the shortest story we can imagine: an object is lost, and then recovered. But even the most complex narratives can be read as variants on this model: the pattern of classical narrative is that an original settlement is disrupted and ultimately restored. From this viewpoint, narrative is a   10 source of consolation: lost objects are a cause of anxiety to us, symbolizing certain deeper unconscious losses (of birth, the faeces, the mother), and it is always pleasurable to find them put securely back in place. In Lacanian theory, it is an original lost object – the mother's body – which drives forward the narrative of our lives, impelling us to pursue   15 substitutes for this lost paradise in the endless metonymic movement of desire. For Freud, it is a desire to scramble back to a place where we cannot be harmed, the inorganic existence which precedes all conscious life, which keeps us struggling forward: our restless attachments (Eros) are in thrall to the death drive (Thanatos). Something must be lost or   20 absent in any narrative for it to unfold: if everything stayed in place there would be no story to tell. This loss is distressing, but exciting as well: desire is stimulated by what we cannot quite possess, and this is one source of narrative satisfaction. If we could never possess it, however, our excitation might become intolerable and turn into unpleasure; so we   25 must know that the object will be finally restored to us, that Tom Jones will return to Paradise Hall and Hercule Poirot will track down the murderer. Our excitation is gratifyingly released: our energies have been cunningly 'bound' by the suspenses and repetitions of the narrative only as a preparation for their pleasurable expenditure. We have been able to   30 tolerate the disappearance of the object because our unsettling suspense was all the time shot through by the secret knowledge that it would finally come home. *Fort* has meaning only in relation to *da*.

Terry Eagleton: *Literary Theory: An Introduction*

2 Try and apply the principle 'something lost – something restored' to any two or three stories from your own literature. Work with another student. Outline the story in very simple terms, and explain how the principle applies.

Background VII

The final extract is from *The White Hotel* by D. M. Thomas. This is again fiction, but the section from which this extract is taken purports to be a case history written by Freud himself, and indeed the author has managed to achieve a prose style remarkably similar to Freud's. It is included here as part of the sequence and as an indication of how a contemporary author may assume his readers are familiar with the 'ideas' behind the text of this section.

1 Read the following extract.

IN THE AUTUMN of 1919 I was asked by a doctor of my acquaintance to examine a young lady who had been suffering for the past four years from severe pains in her left breast and pelvic region, as well as a chronic respiratory condition. When making this request he added that he thought the case was one of   5
hysteria, though there were certain counter-indications which had caused him to examine her very thoroughly indeed in order to rule out the possibility of some organic affection. The young woman was married, but living apart from her husband, in the home of an aunt. Our patient had had a promising musical career   10
interrupted by her illness.

My first interview of this young woman of twenty-nine years of age did not help me to make much progress in understanding her case, nor could I glimpse any sign of the inner vitality I was assured she possessed. Her face, in which the eyes were the best   15
feature, showed the marks of severe physical suffering; yet there were moments when it registered nothing, and at these times I was reminded of the faces of victims of battle traumas, whom it had been my melancholy duty to examine. When she talked, it was often difficult for me to hear, on account of her hoarse and   20
rapid breathing. As a consequence of her pains, she walked with an awkward gait, bending forward from the waist. She was extremely thin, even by the standards of that unhappy year, when few in Vienna had enough to eat. I suspected an anorexia nervosa, on top of her other troubles. She told me the mere   25
thought of food made her ill, and she was living on oranges and water.

On examining her I understood my colleague's reluctance to abandon the search for an organic basis for her symptoms. I was struck by the definiteness of all the descriptions of the character of   30
her pains given me by the patient, the kind of response we have come to expect from a patient suffering from an organic illness – unless he is neurotic in addition. The hysteric will tend to describe his pain indefinitely, and will tend to respond to stimulation of the painful part rather with an expression of   35

pleasure than pain. Frau Anna, on the contrary, indicated where she hurt precisely and calmly: her left breast and left ovary; and flinched and drew back from my examination.

She herself was convinced that her symptoms were organic and was very disappointed that I could not find the cause and put it right. My own increasing conviction that I was, despite appearances to the contrary, dealing with an hysteria was confirmed when she confessed that she also suffered from visual hallucinations of a disordered and frightening nature. She had feared to confess to these "storms in her head", because it seemed to her an admission that she was mad and should be locked away. I was able to assure her that her hallucinations, like her pains and her breathing difficulties, were no sign of dementia; that indeed, given the intractable nature of reality, the healthiest mind may become a prey to hysterical symptoms. Her manner thereafter became a little more relaxed, and she was able to tell me something of the history of her illness and of her life in general. . .

. . . .

The patient had the fondest memories of her mother. She possessed a warmly maternal nature, handsome looks, a creative spirit (she was a water-colourist of some talent), and an impulsive gaiety. If she had grey moods, usually in response to miserable autumn or winter weather, she indulged her children all the more when they were over. She and Anna's father made a handsome couple. The father also had great energy and charm, and the children adored him though she wished he were not so busy. He had worked immensely hard, without parental support, to establish himself in business. Shortly after Anna's birth, he had moved his family to Odessa, where he became the owner of a grain-exporting firm. Almost his only relaxation was sailing: he was the proud owner of a splendid yacht.

D. M. Thomas: *The White Hotel*

2 What evidence can you find that the narrator ('I') in the above is meant to be the same person as Freud in the extract in *VI* above.

3 From what you have already read about Freud, how does this case history represent his ideas about the nature of mental illness?

SUMMARY OF THE UNIT

1 This unit has focused on a wide range of factors which can influence how we interpret a text.

2 The general term used is 'background'. This can include details of the life and experience of the writer as well as social, historical, political and psychological

143

factors. There will almost certainly be a number of relevant background facts in connection with each text you study.

3 This book has adopted mainly language-based approaches. We think language is central to our understanding of literature but there is always more to a text than its language. We hope you will be encouraged to re-read some of the texts we have examined in previous units in order to discover more about their 'background'.

Unit 10   In the forum: Reading and discussing literature

Introduction for the student

In this unit the starting point for discussion is the literary text itself rather than its background. There are samples from drama, prose, and poetry and the discussion centres on the characters' 'view of life' as revealed by their actions and words. We will ask you to make an intellectual or moral judgement on this view. With careful reading of the text you should work out your own views on the subject clearly first. You will then be asked to take sides and argue a case 'for' and 'against'.

This unit should provide you with a basis for saying what you think about a text. The previous units should have helped you to read, study and analyse so that you can support your views with close reference to the text.

Forum I

The texts in *Forum I* and *II* are both from plays by Shakespeare.
The following extract is from *Henry IV* Part 1. Falstaff is one of Shakespeare's most memorable characters, and here he gives his views on honour. (Here honouring one's country is synonymous with loyalty.) Falstaff is amiable, boastful, drunken and a coward. But in general we (the audience) like him, because we see in him weaknesses which exist in all of us. So do not condemn him too quickly, for he is very 'human'.

1 The threat of civil war hangs over England. 'It' (the first word of the text) refers to an offer to reach an agreement.
Now read on.

> *Prince.* It will not be accepted, on my life;
>   The Douglas and the Hotspur both together
>   Are confident against the world in arms.
> *King.* Hence, therefore, every leader to his charge;
>   For on their answer will we set on them,   5
>   And God befriend us as our cause is just!
>   *Exeunt all but the Prince and Falstaff.*
> *Fal.* Hal, if thou see me down in the battle and bestride me, so; 'tis a
>   point of friendship.

Prince. Nothing but a Colossus can do thee that friendship. Say thy
    prayers, and farewell.   10
Fal. I would 'twere bed-time, Hal, and all well.
Prince. Why, thou owest God a death.   *Exit*
Fal. 'Tis not due yet, I would be loath to pay him before his day—what
    need I be so forward with him that calls not on me? Well, 'tis no
    matter, honour pricks me on. Yea, but how if honour prick me off   15
    when I come on, how then? Can honour set to a leg? No. Or an arm?
    No. Or take away the grief of a wound? No. Honour hath no skill in
    surgery then? No. What is honour? A word. What is in that word
    honour? What is that honour? Air. A trim reckoning! Who hath it?
    He that died a-Wednesday. Doth he feel it? No. Doth he hear it?   20
    No. 'Tis insensible, then? Yea, to the dead. But will it not live with
    the living? No. Why? Detraction will not suffer it. Therefore I'll
    none of it. Honour is a mere scutcheon—and so ends my catechism.

                                             Exit

    William Shakespeare: *Henry IV* Part 1 (*V, i*)

2 Divide into groups of six. Then divide into sub-groups of three and appoint a
spokesperson in each sub-group. Toss a coin ('heads' or 'tails') for sides – the
winning side having the choice of topic, as follows:

    A *Falstaff is right.* Honour is fine, but it is not much satisfaction if you
      are dead, to you or your relatives.

    B *Falstaff is wrong.* The world would just collapse into anarchy if we
      were not prepared to defend the honour of our country, our family
      and our own person.

Prepare for 10 minutes, and then the spokesperson for each group presents one
side of the debate. Argument A (Falstaff is right) is presented first. Speakers from
the opposition may interrupt if the spokesperson allows it.

3 Resume your groups of six. Discuss, informally, the application of Falstaff's
speech to the world debate on nuclear weapons, and nuclear disarmament.

Forum II

1 The second extract is from Shakespeare's tragedy *Othello*. In this section the text
is given first. Read it carefully.

        Iago.   I do beseech you,
           Though I perchance am vicious in my guess,

(As I confess it is my nature's plague
To spy into abuses, and oft my jealousy
Shapes faults that are not) I entreat you then,   5
From one that so imperfectly conjects,
You'ld take no notice, nor build yourself a trouble
Out of my scattering and unsure observance;
It were not for your quiet, nor your good,
Nor for my manhood, honesty, or wisdom,   10
To let you know my thoughts.

Oth.   Zounds!

Iago. Good name in man and woman's dear, my lord;
Is the immediate jewel of our souls:
Who steals my purse, steals trash, 'tis something, nothing,
'Twas mine, 'tis his, and has been slave to thousands: 15
But he that filches from me my good name
Robs me of that which not enriches him,
And makes me poor indeed.

Oth. By heaven I'll know thy thought.

Iago. You cannot, if my heart were in your hand,   20
Nor shall not, whilst 'tis in my custody:
O, beware jealousy;
It is the green-ey'd monster, which doth mock
That meat it feeds on. That cuckold lives in bliss,
Who, certain of his fate, loves not his wronger: 25
But O, what damned minutes tells he o'er
Who dotes, yet doubts, suspects, yet strongly loves!

Oth. O misery!

Iago. Poor and content is rich, and rich enough,
But riches, fineless, is as poor as winter   30
To him that ever fears he shall be poor:
Good God, the souls of all my tribe defend
From jealousy!

Oth.   Why, why is this?
Think'st though I'ld make a life of jealousy?
To follow still the changes of the moon   35
With fresh suspicions? No, to be once in doubt,
Is once to be resolv'd: exchange me for a goat,
When I shall turn the business of my soul
To such exsufflicate and blown surmises,
Matching thy inference: 'tis not to make me jealous,   40
To say my wife is fair, feeds well, loves company,
Is free of speech, sings, plays, and dances well;
Where virtue is, these are more virtuous:
Nor from mine own weak merits will I draw
The smallest fear, or doubt of her revolt,   45
For she had eyes, and chose me. No, Iago,

I'll see before I doubt, when I doubt, prove,
And on the proof, there is no more but this:
Away at once with love or jealousy!

Iago. I am glad of it, for now I shall have reason   50
To show the love and duty that I bear you
With franker spirit: therefore as I am bound
Receive it from me: I speak not yet of proof;
Look to your wife, observe her well with Cassio;
Wear your eye thus, not jealous, nor secure.   55
I would not have your free and noble nature
Out of self-bounty be abused, look to 't:
I know our country disposition well;
In Venice they do let God see the pranks
They dare not show their husbands: their best conscience   60
Is not to leave undone, but keep unknown.

Oth. Dost thou say so?

Iago. She did deceive her father, marrying you;
And when she seem'd to shake and fear your looks,
She lov'd them most.   65

Oth.   And so she did.

Iago.   Why, go to then,
She that so young could give out such a seeming,
To seal her father's eyes up, close as oak,
He thought 'twas witchcraft: but I am much to blame,
I humbly do beseech you of your pardon,
For too much loving you.   70

Oth.   I am bound to thee for ever.

Iago. I see this hath a little dash'd your spirits.

Oth. Not a jot, not a jot.

Iago.   I' faith I fear it has.
I hope you will consider what is spoke
Comes from my love: but I do see you are mov'd,
I am to pray you, not to strain my speech   75
To grosser issues, nor to larger reach,
Than to suspicion.

Oth. I will not.

Iago.   Should you do so, my lord,
My speech should fall into such vile success
As my thoughts aim not at: Cassio's my trusty friend: 80
My lord, I see you are mov'd.

Oth.   No, not much mov'd,
I do not think but Desdemona's honest.

Iago. Long live she so, and long live you to think so!

Oth. And yet how nature erring from itself—

Iago. Ay, there's the point: as, to be bold with you,   85
Not to affect many proposed matches,

Of her own clime, complexion, and degree,
Whereto we see in all things nature tends;
Fie, we may smell in such a will most rank,
Foul disproportion; thoughts unnatural.   90
But pardon me: I do not in position
Distinctly speak of her, though I may fear
Her will, recoiling to her better judgement,
May fall to match you with her country forms,
And happily repent.   95
Oth.   Farewell, if more
Thou dost perceive, let me know more, set on
Thy wife to observe; leave me, Iago.
Iago. [*Going*] My lord, I take my leave.
Oth. Why did I marry? This honest creature doubtless
Sees and knows more, much more, than he unfolds.   100
Iago. [*Returning*] My lord, I would I might entreat your honour
To scan this thing no further, leave it to time:
Though it be fit that Cassio have his place,
For sure he fills it up with great ability,
Yet if you please to hold him off awhile,   105
You shall by that perceive him and his means;
Note if your lady strain her entertainment
With any strong or vehement importunity,
Much will be seen in that; in the mean time,
Let me be thought too busy in my fears   110
(As worthy cause I have to fear I am);
And hold her free, I do beseech your honour.
Oth. Fear not my government.
Iago. I once more take my leave.   *Exit*
Oth. This fellow's of exceeding honesty,   115
And knows all qualities, with a learned spirit,
Of human dealing: if I do prove her haggard,
Though that her jesses were my dear heart-strings,
I'ld whistle her off, and let her down the wind,
To prey at fortune. Haply, for I am black,   120
And have not those soft parts of conversation
That chamberers have, or for I am declin'd
Into the vale of years,—yet that's not much—
She's gone, I am abus'd, and my relief
Must be to loathe her: O curse of marriage,   125
That we can call these delicate creatures ours,
And not their appetites! I had rather be a toad,
And live upon the vapour in a dungeon,
Than keep a corner in a thing I love,
For others' uses . . .   130

William Shakespeare: *Othello* (III, iii)

2 Working individually find out the plot of *Othello*. You are not asked to read the play. Your investigation is a personal task, using library facilities or other resources.

In the above extract Othello is apparently concerned about honour, at the personal level, though whether his own or Desdemona's is a difficult question to answer, as the complex matter of male–female relations and emotions is also involved.

The question to be resolved is whether you, in Othello's position would be convinced by what Iago says (see the discussion topics in number 3 below).

a) Listen to the recording of this exchange between Othello and Iago. Use the categories from Unit 4 *Orientation* to help you to work out how the words were spoken.

b) Working in groups of six, create a scenario for this scene (see Unit 2).

c) Still in groups, make a brief summary of each of the longer speeches by the two characters. Discuss and reach agreement before writing anything. At the end of this you should have a clear idea of each step in the interaction between the two characters, even if you do not understand every word. You may if you wish reconstruct the scene as a brief dialogue in modern English.

d) As in the ranking exercises in Unit 3 make a list of statements about the interaction, with a line reference so that you can trace it back to the text. For example:

>   Iago admits that he is a busybody. (l. 50)
>   Iago tells Othello to take no notice of his (Iago's) suspicions.

Spend as much time on this as you need, as it will help you in the debate activity which follows. You are not required to rank the statements.

3 This activity needs preparation, but steps (a) to (d) above will help you. Divide into sub-groups of three, and appoint a spokesperson in each sub-group. Decide on sides to discuss the following topics:

>   A Iago is a trusted associate and Othello does not need to question what he says.

>   B It is inevitable that Othello will be deeply worried by what Iago says.

EXPLOITATION

Iago, speaking of Desdemona, says:

>   . . . I may fear
>   Her will . . .
>   May fall to match you with her country forms,
>   And happily repent.

Note: 'happily' here probably means 'readily'.

Resume your groups of six. Discuss, informally, whether 'mixed' marriages, between black and white, or partners of widely separated cultures, are more likely to fail. Do you think Iago is correct or mistaken when he says that, when things go wrong, one partner is likely to compare the other unfavourably with others of his or her own colour or nationality?

Forum III

We now turn to prose, and the first example is a complete short story, not an extract. It is 'The Force of Circumstance' by W. Somerset Maugham (1874–1965) (see also Unit 7, pp. 102, 104–5). The setting is Malaysia (then called Malaya) and the period about 1925.

The reading task should be undertaken ahead of the classroom activity.

The task is slightly different here. You are given the discussion topics before you begin reading, and you should refer back to them frequently as the story develops. You do not, of course, know which side you will defend.

The topics for discussion are as follows:

A   Guy is wrong. He should have told Doris about his past before he married her.

B   Doris is wrong. She should have forgiven Guy for his honesty and sincerity and responded to his love and kindness.

1   Read the story. Do not take any notice of the shaded areas at this stage.

W. Somerset Maugham
THE FORCE OF CIRCUMSTANCE

SHE was sitting on the veranda waiting for her husband to come in for luncheon. The Malay boy had drawn the blinds when the morning lost its freshness, but she had partly raised one of them so that she could look at the river. Under the breathless sun of midday it had the white pallor of death. A native was paddling ⁵ along in a dug-out so small that it hardly showed above the surface of the water. The colours of the day were ashy and wan. They were but the various tones of the heat. (It was like an Eastern melody, in the minor key, which exacerbates the nerves by its ambiguous monotony; and the ear awaits impatiently a ¹⁰ resolution, but waits in vain.) The cicadas sang their grating song with a frenzied energy; it was as continual and monotonous as the rustling of a brook over the stones; but on a sudden it was drowned by the loud singing of a bird, mellifluous and rich; and for an instant, with a catch at her heart, she thought of the English ¹⁵ blackbird.

Then she heard her husband's step on the gravel path behind the bungalow, the path that led to the court-house in which he had been working, and she rose from her chair to greet him. He ran up the short flight of steps, for the bungalow was built on ²⁰ piles, and at the door the boy was waiting to take his topee. He came into the room which served them as a dining-room and parlour, and his eyes lit up with pleasure as he saw her.

'Hulloa, Doris. Hungry?'

'Ravenous.' ²⁵

'It'll only take me a minute to have a bath and then I'm ready.'

'Be quick,' she smiled.

He disappeared into his dressing-room and she heard him whistling cheerily while, with the carelessness with which she was always remonstrating, he tore off his clothes and flung them ³⁰

152

on the floor. He was twenty-nine, but he was still a school-boy; he
would never grow up. That was why she had fallen in love with
him, perhaps, for no amount of affection could persuade her that
he was good-looking. He was a little round man, with a red face
like the full moon, and blue eyes. He was rather pimply. She had   35
examined him carefully and had been forced to confess to him
that he had not a single feature which she could praise. She had
told him often that he wasn't her type at all.

'I never said I was a beauty,' he laughed.

'I can't think what it is I see in you.'   40

But of course she knew perfectly well. He was a gay, jolly little
man, who took nothing very solemnly, and he was constantly
laughing. He made her laugh too. He found life an amusing
rather than a serious business, and he had a charming smile.
When she was with him she felt happy and good-tempered. And   45
the deep affection which she saw in those merry blue eyes of his
touched her. It was very satisfactory to be loved like that. Once,
sitting on his knees, during their honeymoon she had taken his
face in her hands and said to him:

'You're an ugly, little fat man, Guy, but you've got charm. I   50
can't help loving you.'

A wave of emotion swept over her and her eyes filled with
tears. She saw his face contorted for a moment with the extremity
of his feeling and his voice was a little shaky when he answered.

'It's a terrible thing for me to have married a woman who's   55
mentally deficient,' he said.

She chuckled. It was the characteristic answer which she would
have liked him to make.

It was hard to realize that nine months ago she had never even
heard of him. She had met him at a small place by the seaside   60
where she was spending a month's holiday with her mother.
Doris was a secretary to a member of parliament, Guy was home
on leave. They were staying at the same hotel, and he quickly told
her all about himself. He was born in Sembulu, where his father
had served for thirty years under the second Sultan, and on   65
leaving school he had entered the same service. He was devoted
to the country.

'After all, England's a foreign land to me,' he told her. 'My
home's Sembulu.'

And now it was her home too. He asked her to marry him at the   70
end of the month's holiday. She had known he was going to, and
had decided to refuse him. She was her widowed mother's only
child and she could not go so far away from her, but when the
moment came she did not quite know what happened to her, she
was carried off her feet by an unexpected emotion, and she   75
accepted him. They had been settled now for four months in

153

the little outstation of which he was in charge. She was very happy.

She told him once that she had quite made up her mind to refuse him. 80

'Are you sorry you didn't?' he asked, with a merry smile in his twinkling blue eyes.

'I should have been a perfect fool if I had. What a bit of luck that fate or chance or whatever it was stepped in and took the matter entirely out of my hands!' 85

Now she heard Guy clatter down the steps to the bath-house. He was a noisy fellow and even with bare feet he could not be quiet. But he uttered an exclamation. He said two or three words in the local dialect and she could not understand. Then she heard someone speaking to him, not aloud, but in a sibilant whisper. 90 Really it was too bad of people to waylay him when he was going to have his bath. He spoke again and though his voice was low she could hear that he was vexed. The other voice was raised now; it was a woman's. Doris supposed it was someone who had a complaint to make. It was like a Malay woman to come in that 95 surreptitious way. But she was evidently getting very little from Guy, for she heard him say: Get out. That at all events she understood, and then she heard him bolt the door. There was a sound of the water he was throwing over himself (the bathing arrangements still amused her; the bath-houses were under the 100 bedrooms, on the ground; you had a large tub of water and you sluiced yourself with a little tin pail) and in a couple of minutes he was back again in the dining-room. His hair was still wet. They sat down to luncheon.

'It's lucky I'm not a suspicious or a jealous person,' she 105 laughed. 'I don't know that I should altogether approve of your having animated conversations with ladies while you're having your bath.'

His face, usually so cheerful, had borne a sullen look when he came in, but now it brightened. 110

'I wasn't exactly pleased to see her.'

'So I judged by the tone of your voice. In fact, I thought you were rather short with the young person.'

'Damned cheek, waylaying me like that!'

'What did she want?' 115

'Oh, I don't know. It's a woman from the kampong. She's had a row with her husband or something.'

'I wonder if it's the same one who was hanging about this morning.'

He frowned a little. 120

'Was there someone hanging about?'

'Yes, I went into your dressing-room to see that everything was

nice and tidy, and then I went down to the bath-house. I saw
someone slink out of the door as I went down the steps and when
I looked out I saw a woman standing there.'   125
'Did you speak to her?'
'I asked her what she wanted and she said something, but I
couldn't understand.'
'I'm not going to have all sorts of stray people prowling about
here,' he said. 'They've got no right to come.'   130
He smiled, but Doris, with the quick perception of a woman in
love, noticed that he smiled only with his lips, not as usual with
his eyes also, and wondered what it was that troubled him.
'What have you been doing this morning?' he asked.
'Oh, nothing much. I went for a little walk.'   135
'Through the kampong?'
'Yes. I saw a man send a chained monkey up a tree to pick
coconuts, which rather thrilled me.'
'It's rather a lark, isn't it?'
'Oh, Guy, there were two little boys watching him who were   140
much whiter than the others. I wondered if they were half-castes.
I spoke to them, but they didn't know a word of English.'

II   'There are two or three half-caste children in the kampong,' he
answered.
'Who do they belong to?'   145
'Their mother is one of the village girls.'
'Who is their father?'
'Oh, my dear, that's the sort of question we think it a little
dangerous to ask out here.' He paused. 'A lot of fellows have
native wives, and then when they go home or marry they pension   150
them off and send them back to their village.'
Doris was silent. The indifference with which he spoke seemed
a little callous to her. There was almost a frown on her frank,
open, pretty English face when she replied.
'But what about the children?'   155
'I have no doubt they're properly provided for. Within his
means, a man generally sees that there's enough money to have
them decently educated. They get jobs as clerks in a government
office, you know; they're all right.'
She gave him a slightly rueful smile.   160
'You can't expect me to think it's a very good system.'
'You mustn't be too hard,' he smiled back.
'I'm not hard. But I'm thankful you never had a Malay wife. I
should have hated it. Just think if those two little brats were
yours.'   165
The boy changed their plates. There was never much variety in
their menu. They started luncheon with river fish, dull and
insipid, so that a good deal of tomato ketchup was needed to

make it palatable, and then went on to some kind of stew. Guy
poured Worcester Sauce over it.   170

'The old Sultan didn't think it was a white woman's country,'
he said presently. 'He rather encouraged people to – keep house
with native girls. Of course things have changed now. The
country's perfectly quiet and I suppose we know better how to
cope with the climate.'   175

'But, Guy, the eldest of those boys wasn't more than seven or
eight and the other was about five.'

'It's awfully lonely on an outstation. Why, often one doesn't
see another white man for six months on end. A fellow comes out
here when he's only a boy.' He gave her that charming smile of   180
his which transfigured his round, plain face. 'There are excuses,
you know.'

She always found that smile irresistible. It was his best
argument. Her eyes grew once more soft and tender.

'I'm sure there are.' She stretched her hand across the little   185
table and put it on his. 'I'm very lucky to have caught you so
young. Honestly, it would upset me dreadfully if I were told that
you had lived like that.'

He took her hand and pressed it.

'Are you happy here, darling'?   190

'Desperately.'

She looked very cool and fresh in her linen frock. The heat did
not distress her. She had no more than the prettiness of youth,
though her brown eyes were fine; but she had a pleasing
frankness of expression, and her dark, short hair was neat and   195
glossy. She gave you the impression of a girl of spirit and you felt
sure that the member of parliament for whom she worked had in
her a very competent secretary.

'I loved the country at once,' she said. 'Although I'm alone so
much I don't think I've ever once felt lonely.'   200

Of course she had read novels about the Malay Archipelago
and she had formed an impression of a sombre land with great
ominous rivers and a silent, impenetrable jungle. When the little
coasting steamer set them down at the mouth of the river, where
a large boat, manned by a dozen Dyaks, was waiting to take them 205
to the station, her breath was taken away by the beauty, friendly
rather than awe-inspiring, of the scene. It had a gaiety, like the
joyful singing of birds in the trees, which she had never expected.
On each bank of the river were mangroves and nipah palms, and
behind them the dense green of the forest. In the distance   210
stretched blue mountains, range upon range, as far as the eye
could see. She had no sense of confinement nor of gloom, but
rather of openness and wide spaces where the exultant fancy
could wander with delight. The green glittered in the sunshine

and then the sky was blithe and cheerful. The gracious land 215
seemed to offer her a smiling welcome.

They rowed on, hugging a bank, and high overhead flew a pair
of doves. A flash of colour, like a living jewel, dashed across their
path. It was a kingfisher. Two monkeys, with their dangling tails,
sat side by side on a branch. On the horizon, over there on the 220
other side of the broad and turbid river, beyond the jungle, was a
row of little white clouds, the only clouds in the sky, and they
looked like a row of ballet-girls, dressed in white, waiting at the
back of the stage, alert and merry, for the curtain to go up. Her
heart was filled with joy; and now, remembering it all, her eyes 225
rested on her husband with a grateful, assured affection.

And what fun it had been to arrange their living-room! It was
very big. On the floor, when she arrived, was torn and dirty
matting; on the walls of unpainted wood hung (much too high
up) photogravures of Academy pictures, Dyak shields, and 230
parangs. The tables were covered with Dyak cloth in sombre
colours, and on them stood pieces of Brunei brassware, much in
need of cleaning, empty cigarette tins, and bits of Malay silver.
There was a rough wooden shelf with cheap editions of novels
and a number of old travel books in battered leather; and another 235
shelf was crowded with empty bottles. It was a bachelor's room,
untidy but stiff; and though it amused her she found it intolerably
pathetic. It was a dreary, comfortless life that Guy had led there,
and she threw her arms round his neck and kissed him.

'You poor darling,' she laughed. 240

She had deft hands and she soon made the room habitable. She
arranged this and that, and what she could not do with she
turned out. Her wedding-presents helped. Now the room was
friendly and comfortable. In glass vases were lovely orchids and
in great bowls huge masses of flowering shrubs. She felt an 245
inordinate pride because it was her house (she had never in her
life lived in anything but a poky flat) and she had made it
charming for him.

'Are you pleased with me?' she asked when she had finished.

'Quite,' he smiled. 250

The deliberate understatement was much to her mind. How
jolly it was that they should understand each other so well! They
were both of them shy of displaying emotion, and it was only at
rare moments that they used with one another anything but
ironic banter. 255

They finished luncheon and he threw himself into a long chair
to have a sleep. She went towards her room. She was a little
surprised that he drew her to him as she passed and, making her
bend down, kissed her lips. They were not in the habit of
exchanging embraces at odd hours of the day. 260

157

'A full tummy is making you sentimental, my poor lamb,' she chaffed him.

'Get out and don't let me see you again for at least two hours.'

'Don't snore.'

She left him. They had risen at dawn and in five minutes were 265 fast asleep.

Doris was awakened by the sound of her husband's splashing in the bath-house. The walls of the bungalow were like a sounding board and not a thing that one of them did escaped the other. She felt too lazy to move, but she heard the boy bring the 270 tea things in, so she jumped up and ran down into her own bath-house. The water, not cold but cool, was deliciously refreshing. When she came into the sitting-room Guy was taking the rackets out of the press, for they played tennis in the short cool of the evening. The night fell at six. 275

The tennis-court was two or three hundred yards from the bungalow and after tea, anxious not to lose time, they strolled down to it.

'Oh, look,' said Doris, 'there's that girl that I saw this morning.'

Guy turned quickly. His eyes rested for a moment on a native 280 woman, but he did not speak.

'What a pretty sarong she's got,' said Doris. 'I wonder where it comes from.'

They passed her. She was slight and small, with the large, dark, starry eyes of her race and a mass of raven hair. She did not 285 stir as they went by, but stared at them strangely. Doris saw then that she was not quite so young as she had at first thought. Her features were a trifle heavy and her skin was dark, but she was very pretty. She held a small child in her arms. Doris smiled a little as she saw it, but no answering smile moved the woman's 290 lips. Her face remained impassive. She did not look at Guy, she looked only at Doris, and he walked on as though he did not see her. Doris turned to him.

'Isn't that baby a duck?'

'I didn't notice.' 295

She was puzzled by the look of his face. It was deathly white, and the pimples which not a little distressed her were more than commonly red.

'Did you notice her hands and feet? She might be a duchess.'

'All natives have good hands and feet,' he answered, but not 300 jovially as was his wont; it was as though he forced himself to speak.

But Doris was intrigued.

'Who is she, d'you know?'

'She's one of the girls in the kampong.' 305

They had reached the court now. When Guy went up to the net

to see that it was taut he looked back. The girl was still standing
where they had passed her. Their eyes met.

'Shall I serve?' said Doris.

'Yes, you've got the balls on your side.'   310

He played very badly. Generally he gave her fifteen and beat
her, but today she won easily. And he played silently. Generally
he was a noisy player, shouting all the time, cursing his
foolishness when he missed a ball and chaffing her when he
placed one out of her reach.   315

'You're off your game, young man,' she cried.

'Not a bit,' he said.

He began to slam the balls, trying to beat her, and sent one after
the other into the net. She had never seen him with that set face.
Was it possible that he was a little out of temper because he was   320
not playing well? The light fell, and they ceased to play. The
woman whom they had passed stood in exactly the same position
as when they came and once more, with expressionless face, as
she watched them go.

The blinds on the veranda were raised now, and on the table   325
between their two long chairs were bottles and soda-water. This
was the hour at which they had the first drink of the day and Guy
mixed a couple of gin slings. The river stretched widely before
them, and on the farther bank the jungle was wrapped in the
mystery of the approaching night. A native was silently rowing   330
up-stream, standing at the bow of the boat, with two oars.

'I played like a fool,' said Guy, breaking a silence. 'I'm feeling a
bit under the weather.'

'I'm sorry. You're not going to have fever, are you?'

'Oh, no. I shall be all right tomorrow.'   335

Darkness closed in upon them. The frogs croaked loudly and
now and then they heard a few short notes from some singing
bird of the night. Fireflies flitted across the veranda and they
made the trees that surrounded it look like Christmas trees lit
with tiny candles. They sparkled softly. Doris thought she heard   340
a little sigh. It vaguely disturbed her. Guy was always so full of
gaiety.

'What is it, old man?' she said gently. 'Tell mother.'

'Nothing. Time for another drink,' he answered breezily.

Next day he was as cheerful as ever and the mail came. The   345
coasting steamer passed the mouth of the river twice a month,
once on its way to the coalfields and once on its way back. On the
outward journey it brought mail, which Guy sent a boat down to
fetch. Its arrival was the excitement of their uneventful lives. For
the first day or two they skimmed rapidly all that had come,   350
letters, English papers and papers from Singapore, magazines
and books, leaving for the ensuing weeks a more exact perusal.

159

They snatched the illustrated papers from one another. If Doris had not been so absorbed she might have noticed that there was a change in Guy. She would have found it hard to describe and 355 harder still to explain. There was in his eyes a sort of watchfulness and in his mouth a slight droop of anxiety.

Then, perhaps a week later, one morning when she was sitting in the shaded room studying a Malay grammar (for she was industriously learning the language) she heard a commotion in 360 the compound. She heard the house boy's voice, he was speaking angrily, the voice of another man, perhaps it was the water-carrier's, and then a woman's, shrill and vituperative. There was a scuffle. She went to the window and opened the shutters. The water-carrier had hold of a woman's arm and was dragging her 365 along, while the house boy was pushing her from behind with both hands. Doris recognized her at once as the woman she had seen one morning loitering in the compound and later in the day outside the tennis-court. She was holding a baby against her breast. All three were shouting angrily. 370

'Stop,' cried Doris. 'What are you doing?'

At the sound of her voice the water-carrier let go suddenly and the woman, still pushed from behind, fell to the ground. There was a sudden silence and the house boy looked sullenly into space. The water-carrier hesitated a moment and then slunk 375 away. The woman raised herself slowly to her feet, arranged the baby on her arm, and stood impassive, staring at Doris. The boy said something to her which Doris could not have heard even if she had understood; the woman by no change of face showed that his words meant anything to her; but she slowly strolled 380 away. The boy followed her to the gate of the compound. Doris called to him as he walked back, but he pretended not to hear. She was growing angry now and she called more sharply.

'Come here at once,' she cried.

III   Suddenly, avoiding her wrathful glance, he came towards the 385 bungalow. He came in and stood at the door. He looked at her sulkily.

'What were you doing with that woman?' she asked abruptly.

'*Tuan* say she no come here.'

'You mustn't treat a woman like that. I won't have it. I shall tell 390 the *tuan* exactly what I saw.'

The boy did not answer. He looked away, but she felt that he was watching her through his long eyelashes. She dismissed him.

'That'll do.' 395

Without a word he turned and went back to the servants' quarters. She was exasperated and she found it impossible to give her attention once more to the Malay exercises. In a little while the

boy came in to lay the cloth for luncheon. On a sudden he went to
the door.   400

'What is it?' she asked.

'*Tuan* just coming.'

He went out to take Guy's hat from him. His quick ears had
caught the footsteps before they were audible to her. Guy did not
as usual come up the steps immediately; he paused, and Doris at   405
once surmised that the boy had gone down to meet him in order
to tell him of the morning's incident. She shrugged her
shoulders. The boy evidently wanted to get his story in first. But
she was astonished when Guy came in. His face was ashy.

'Guy, what on earth's the matter?'   410

He flushed a sudden hot red.

'Nothing. Why?'

She was so taken aback that she let him pass into his room
without a word of what she had meant to speak of at once. It took
him longer than usual to have his bath and change his clothes and 415
luncheon was served when he came in.

'Guy,' she said, as they sat down, 'that woman we saw the
other day was here again this morning.'

'So I've heard,' he answered.

'The boys were treating her brutally. I had to stop them. You   420
must really speak to them about it.'

Though the Malay understood every word she said he made no
sign that he heard. He handed her the toast.

'She's been told not to come here. I gave instructions that if she
showed herself again she was to be turned out.'   425

'Were they obliged to be so rough?'

'She refused to go. I don't think they were any rougher than
they could help.'

'It was horrible to see a woman treated like that. She had a baby
in her arms.'   430

'Hardly a baby. It's three years old.'

'How d'you know?'

'I know all about her. She hasn't the least right to come here
pestering everybody.'

'What does she want?'   435

'She wants to do exactly what she did. She wants to make a
disturbance.'

For a little while Doris did not speak. She was surprised at her
husband's tone. He spoke tersely. He spoke as though all this
were no concern of hers. She thought him a little unkind. He was 440
nervous and irritable.

'I doubt if we shall be able to play tennis this afternoon,' he
said. 'It looks to me as though we were going to have a storm.'

The rain was falling when she awoke and it was impossible to

go out. During tea Guy was silent and abstracted. She got her 445
sewing and began to work. Guy sat down to read such of the
English papers as he had not yet gone through from cover to
cover; but he was restless; he walked up and down the large room
and then went out on the veranda. He looked at the steady rain.
What was he thinking of? Doris was vaguely uneasy. 450

It was not until after dinner that he spoke. During the simple
meal he had exerted himself to be his usual gay self, but the
exertion was apparent. The rain had ceased and the night was
starry. They sat on the veranda. In order not to attract insects they
had put out the lamp in the sitting-room. At their feet, with a 455
mighty, formidable sluggishness, silent, mysterious, and fatal,
flowed the river. It had the terrible deliberation and the
relentlessness of destiny.

IV   'Doris, I've got something to say to you,' he said suddenly.

His voice was very strange. Was it her fancy that he had 460
difficulty in keeping it quite steady? She felt a little pang in her
heart because he was in distress, and she put her hand gently into
his. He drew it away.

'It's rather a long story. I'm afraid it's not a very nice one and I
find it rather difficult to tell. I'm going to ask you not to interrupt 465
me, or to say anything, till I've finished.'

In the darkness she could not see his face, but she felt that it
was haggard. She did not answer. He spoke in a voice so low that
it hardly broke the silence of the night.

'I was only eighteen when I came out here. I came straight from 470
school. I spent three months in Kuala Solor, and then I was sent to
a station up the Sembulu river. Of course there was a Resident
there and his wife. I lived in the court-house, but I used to have
my meals with them and spend the evening with them. I had an
awfully good time. Then the fellow who was here fell ill and had 475
to go home. We were short of men on account of the war and I
was put in charge of this place. Of course I was very young, but I
spoke the language like a native, and they remembered my
father. I was as pleased as punch to be on my own.'

He was silent while he knocked the ashes out of his pipe and 480
refilled it. When he lit a match Doris, without looking at him,
noticed that his hand was unsteady.

'I'd never been alone before. Of course at home there'd been
father and mother and generally an assistant. And then at school
naturally there were always fellows about. On the way out, on 485
the boat, there were people all the time, and at K.S., and the same
at my first post. The people there were almost like my own
people. I seemed always to live in a crowd. I like people. I'm a
noisy blighter. I like to have a good time. All sorts of things make
me laugh and you must have somebody to laugh with. But it was 490

different here. Of course it was all right in the day time: I had my
work and I could talk to the Dyaks. Although they were
head-hunters in those days and now and then I had a bit of
trouble with them, they were an awfully decent lot of fellows. I
got on very well with them. Of course I should have liked a white   495
man to gas to, but they were better than nothing, and it was easier
for me because they didn't look upon me quite as a stranger. I
liked the work too. It was rather lonely in the evening to sit on the
veranda and drink a gin and bitters by myself, but I could read.
And the boys were about. My own boy was called Abdul. He'd   500
known my father. When I got tired of reading I could give him a
shout and have a bit of a jaw with him.

V   'It was the nights that did for me. After dinner the boys shut up
and went away to sleep in the kampong. I was all alone. There
wasn't a sound in the bungalow except now and then the croak of 505
the chik-chak. It used to come out of the silence, suddenly, so that
it made me jump. Over in the kampong I heard the sound of a
gong or fire-crackers. They were having a good time, they
weren't so far away, but I had to stay where I was. I was tired of
reading. I couldn't have been more of a prisoner if I'd been in jail. 510
Night after night it was the same. I tried drinking three or four
whiskies, but it's poor fun drinking alone, and it didn't cheer me
up; it only made me feel rather rotten next day. I tried going to
bed immediately after dinner, but I couldn't sleep. I used to lie in
bed, getting hotter and hotter, and more wide awake, till I didn't 515
know what to do with myself. By George, those nights were long.
D'you know, I got so low, I was so sorry for myself that
sometimes – it makes me laugh now when I think of it, but I was
only nineteen and a half – sometimes I used to cry.

'Then, one evening, after dinner, Abdul had cleared away and 520
was just going off, when he gave a little cough. He said, wasn't I
lonely in the house all night by myself? "Oh, no, that's all right," I
said. I didn't want him to know what a damned fool I was, but I
expect he knew all right. He stood there without speaking, and I
knew he wanted to say something to me. "What is it?" I said.   525
"Spit it out." Then he said that if I'd like to have a girl to come and
live with me he knew one who was willing. She was a very good
girl and he could recommend her. She'd be no trouble and it
would be someone to have about the bungalow. She'd mend my
things for me . . . I felt awfully low. It had been raining all day and 530
I hadn't been able to get any exercise. I knew I shouldn't sleep for
hours. It wouldn't cost me very much money, he said, her people
were poor and they'd be quite satisfied with a small present. Two
hundred Straits dollars. "You look," he said. "If you don't like her
you send her away." I asked him where she was. "She's here," he   535
said. "I call her." He went to the door. She'd been waiting on the

163

steps with her mother. They came in and sat down on the floor. I
gave them some sweets. She was shy, of course, but cool enough,
and when I said something to her she gave me a smile. She was
very young, hardly more than a child, they said she was fifteen. 540
She was awfully pretty, and she had her best clothes on. We
began to talk. She didn't say much, but she laughed a lot when I
chaffed her. Abdul said I'd find she had plenty to say for herself
when she got to know me. He told her to come and sit by me. She
giggled and refused, but her mother told her to come, and I made 545
room for her on the chair. She blushed and laughed, but she
came, and then she snuggled up to me. The boy laughed too.
"You see, she's taken to you already," he said. "Do you want her
to stay?" he asked. "Do you want to?" I said to her. She hid her
face, laughing, on my shoulder. She was very soft and small. 550
"Very well," I said, "let her stay." '
    Guy leaned forward and helped himself to a whisky and soda.
    'May I speak now?' asked Doris.
    'Wait a minute, I haven't finished yet. I wasn't in love with her,
not even at the beginning. I only took her so as to have somebody 555
about the bungalow. I think I should have gone mad if I hadn't, or
else taken to drink. I was at the end of my tether. I was too young
to be quite alone. I was never in love with anyone but you.' He
hesitated a moment. 'She lived here till I went home last year on
leave. It's the woman you've seen hanging about.' 560
    'Yes, I guessed that. She had a baby in her arms. Is that your
child?'
    'Yes. It's a little girl.'
    'Is it the only one?'
    'You saw the two small boys the other day in the kampong. You 565
mentioned them.'
    'She has three children then?'
    'Yes.'
    'It's quite a family you've got.'
    She felt the sudden gesture which her remark forced from him, 570
but he did not speak.
    'Didn't she know that you were married till you suddenly
turned up here with a wife?' asked Doris.
    'She knew I was going to be married.'
    'When?' 575
    'I sent her back to the village before I left here. I told her it was
all over. I gave her what I'd promised. She always knew it was
only a temporary arrangement. I was fed up with it. I told her I
was going to marry a white woman.'
    'But you hadn't even seen me then.' 580
    'No, I know. But I'd made up my mind to marry when I was
home.' He chuckled in his old manner. 'I don't mind telling you

that I was getting rather despondent about it when I met you. I
fell in love with you at first sight and then I knew it was either you
or nobody.'   585

VI   'Why didn't you tell me? Don't you think it would have been
only fair to give me a chance of judging for myself? It might have
occurred to you that it would be rather a shock to a girl to find out
that her husband had lived for ten years with another girl and had
three children.'   590

'I couldn't expect you to understand. The circumstances out
here are peculiar. It's the regular thing. Five men out of six do it. I
thought perhaps it would shock you and I didn't want to lose
you. You see, I was most awfully in love with you. I am now,
darling. There was no reason that you should ever know. I didn't   595
expect to come back here. One seldom goes back to the same
station after home leave. When we came here I offered her money
if she'd go to some other village. First she said she would and
then she changed her mind.'

VII   'Why have you told me now?'   600
'She's been making the most awful scenes. I don't know how
she found out that you knew nothing about it. As soon as she did
she began to blackmail me. I've had to give her an awful lot of
money. I gave orders that she wasn't to be allowed in the
compound. This morning she made that scene just to attract your   605
attention. She wanted to frighten me. It couldn't go on like that. I
thought the only thing was to make a clean breast of it.'

There was a long silence as he finished. At last he put his hand
on hers.

'You do understand, Doris, don't you. I know I've been to   610
blame.'

She didn't move her hand. He felt it cold beneath his.

'Is she jealous?'

'I dare say there were all sorts of perks when she was living
here, and I don't suppose she much likes not getting them any   615
longer. But she was never in love with me any more than I was in
love with her. Native women never do really care for white men,
you know.'

'And the children?'

'Oh, the children are all right. I've provided for them. As soon   620
as the boys are old enough I shall send them to school at
Singapore.'

'Do they mean nothing to you at all?'

He hesitated.

'I want to be quite frank with you. I should be sorry if anything   625
happened to them. When the first one was expected I thought I'd
be much fonder of it than I ever had been of its mother. I suppose I
should have been if it had been white. Of course, when it was a

baby it was rather funny and touching, but I had no particular
feeling that it was mine. I think that's what it is; you see, I have no   630
sense of their belonging to me. I've reproached myself sometimes
because it seemed rather unnatural, but the honest truth is that
they're no more to me than if they were somebody else's children.
Of course a lot of slush is talked about children by people who
haven't got any.'   635

Now she had heard everything. He waited for her to speak, but
she said nothing. She sat motionless.

'Is there anything more you want to ask me, Doris?' he said at
last.

'No, I've got rather a headache. I think I shall go to bed.' Her   640
voice was as steady as ever. 'I don't quite know what to say. Of
course it's been all very unexpected. You must give me a little
time to think.'

'Are you very angry with me?'

'No. Not at all. Only – only I must be left to myself for a while.   645
Don't move. I'm going to bed.'

She rose from her long chair and put her hand on his shoulder.

'It's so very hot tonight. I wish you'd sleep in your dressing-
room. Good night.'

She was gone. He heard her lock the door of her bedroom.   650

She was pale next day and he could see that she had not slept.
There was no bitterness in her manner, she talked as usual, but
without ease; she spoke of this and that as though she were
making conversation with a stranger. They had never had a
quarrel, but it seemed to Guy that so would she talk if they had   655
had a disagreement and the subsequent reconciliation had left
her still wounded. The look in her eyes puzzled him; he seemed
to read in them a strange fear. Immediately after dinner she
said:

'I'm not feeling very well tonight. I think I shall go straight to   660
bed.'

'Oh, my poor darling, I'm so sorry,' he cried.

'It's nothing. I shall be all right in a day or two.'

'I shall come in and say good night to you later.'

'No, don't do that. I shall try and get straight off to sleep.'   665

'Well, then, kiss me before you go.'

He saw that she flushed. For an instant she seemed to hesitate;
then, with averted eyes, she leaned towards him. He took her in
his arms and sought her lips, but she turned her face away and he
kissed her cheek. She left him quickly and again he heard the key   670
turn softly in the lock of her door. He flung himself heavily on the
chair. He tried to read, but his ear was attentive to the smallest
sound in his wife's room. She had said she was going to bed, but
he did not hear her move. The silence in there made him

unaccountably nervous. Shading the lamp with his hand he saw   675
that there was a glimmer under her door; she had not put out her
light. What on earth was she doing? He put down his book. It
would not have surprised him if she had been angry and had
made him a scene, or if she had cried; he could have coped with
that; but her calmness frightened him. And then what was that   680
fear which he had seen so plainly in her eyes? He thought once
more over all he had said to her on the previous night. He didn't
know how else he could have put it. After all, the chief point was
that he'd done the same as everybody else, and it was all over
long before he met her. Of course as things turned out he had   685
been a fool, but anyone could be wise after the event. He put his
hand to his heart. Funny how it hurt him there.

'I suppose that's the sort of thing people mean when they say
they're heartbroken,' he said to himself. 'I wonder how long it's
going on like this?'   690

Should he knock at the door and tell her he must speak to her?
It was better to have it out. He *must* make her understand. But the
silence scared him. Not a sound! Perhaps it was better to leave her
alone. Of course it had been a shock. He must give her as long as
she wanted. After all, she knew how devotedly he loved her.   695
Patience, that was the only thing; perhaps she was fighting it out
with herself; he must give her time; he must have patience. Next
morning he asked her if she had slept better.

'Yes, much,' she said.

'Are you very angry with me?' he asked piteously.   700

She looked at him with candid, open eyes.

'Not a bit.'

'Oh, my dear, I'm so glad. I've been a brute and a beast. I know
it's been hateful for you. But do forgive me. I've been so
miserable.'   705

'I do forgive you. I don't even blame you.'

He gave her a little rueful smile, and there was in his eyes the
look of a whipped dog.

'I haven't much liked sleeping by myself the last two nights.'

She glanced away. Her face grew a trifle paler.   710

VIII   'I've had the bed in my room taken away. It took up so much
space. I've had a little camp bed put there instead.'

'My dear, what are you talking about?'

Now she looked at him steadily.

'I'm not going to live with you as your wife again.'   715

'Never?'

She shook her head. He looked at her in a puzzled way. He
could hardly believe he had heard aright and his heart began to
beat painfully.

'But that's awfully unfair to me, Doris.'   720

167

'Don't you think it was a little unfair to me to bring me out here in the circumstances?'

'But you just said you didn't blame me.'

'That's quite true. But the other's different. I can't do it.'

'But how are we going to live together like that?'   725

She stared at the floor. She seemed to ponder deeply.

'When you wanted to kiss me on the lips last night I – it almost made me sick.'

'Doris.'

She looked at him suddenly and her eyes were cold and hostile.   730

'That bed I slept on, is that the bed in which she had her children?' She saw him flush deeply. 'Oh, it's horrible. How could you?' She wrung her hands, and her twisting, tortured fingers looked like little writhing snakes. But she made a great effort and controlled herself. 'My mind is quite made up. I don't   735 want to be unkind to you, but there are some things that you can't ask me to do. I've thought it all over. I've been thinking of nothing else since you told me, night and day, till I'm exhausted. My first instinct was to get up and go. At once. The steamer will be here in two or three days.'   740

'Doesn't it mean anything to you that I love you?'

'Oh, I know you love me. I'm not going to do that. I want to give us both a chance. I have loved you so, Guy.' Her voice broke, but she did not cry. 'I don't want to be unreasonable. Heaven knows, I don't want to be unkind. Guy, will you give me time?'   745

'I don't know quite what you mean.'

'I just want you to leave me alone. I'm frightened by the feelings that I have.'

He had been right then; she was afraid.

'What feelings?'   750

IX   'Please don't ask me. I don't want to say anything to wound you. Perhaps I shall get over them. Heaven knows, I want to. I'll try, I promise you. I'll try. Give me six months. I'll do everything in the world for you, but just that one thing.' She made a little gesture of appeal. 'There's no reason why we shouldn't be happy   755 enough together. If you really love me you'll – you'll have patience.'

He sighed deeply.

'Very well,' he said. 'Naturally I don't want to force you to do anything you don't like. It shall be as you say.'   760

He sat heavily for a little, as though, on a sudden grown old, it was an effort to move; then he got up.

'I'll be getting along to the office.'

He took his topee and went out.

A month passed. Women conceal their feelings better than   765 men and a stranger visiting them would never have guessed that

Doris was in any way troubled. But in Guy the strain was obvious; his round, good-natured face was drawn, and in his eyes was a hungry, harassed look. He watched Doris. She was gay and she chaffed him as she had been used to do; they played tennis 770 together; they chatted about one thing and another. But it was evident that she was merely playing a part, and at last, unable to contain himself, he tried to speak again of his connexions with the Malay woman.

'Oh, Guy, there's no object in going back on all that,' she 775 answered breezily. 'We've said all we had to say about it and I don't blame you for anything.'

'Why do you punish me then?'

'My poor boy, I don't want to punish you. It's not my fault if . . .' she shrugged her shoulders. 'Human nature is very 780 odd.'

'I don't understand.'

'Don't try.'

The words might have been harsh, but she softened them with a pleasant, friendly smile. Every night when she went to bed she 785 leaned over Guy and lightly kissed his cheek. Her lips only touched it. It was as though a moth had just brushed his face in its flight.

A second month passed, then a third, and suddenly the six months which had seemed so interminable were over. Guy asked 790 himself whether she remembered. He gave a strained attention now to everything she said, to every look on her face and to every gesture of her hands. She remained impenetrable. She had asked him to give her six months; well, he had.

The coasting steamer passed the mouth of the river, dropped 795 their mail, and went on its way. Guy busily wrote the letters which it would pick up on the return journey. Two or three days passed by. It was a Tuesday and the *prahu* was to start at dawn on Thursday to await the steamer. Except at meal time when Doris exerted herself to make conversation they had not of late talked 800 very much together; and after dinner as usual they took their books and began to read; but when the boy had finished clearing away and was gone for the night Doris put down hers.

'Guy, I have something I want to say to you,' she murmured.

His heart gave a sudden thud against his ribs and he felt 805 himself change colour.

'Oh, my dear, don't look like that, it's not so very terrible,' she laughed.

But he thought her voice trembled a little.

'Well?'

810

X   'I want you to do something for me.'

'My darling, I'll do anything in the world for you.'

169

He put out his hand to take hers, but she drew it away.

'I want you to let me go home.'

'You?' he cried, aghast. 'When? Why?' 815

'I've borne it as long as I can. I'm at the end of my tether.'

'How long do you want to go for? For always?'

'I don't know. I think so.' She gathered determination. 'Yes, for always.'

'Oh, my God!' 820

His voice broke and she thought he was going to cry.

'Oh, Guy, don't blame me. It really is not my fault. I can't help myself.'

'You asked me for six months. I accepted your terms. You can't say I've made a nuisance of myself.' 825

'No, no.'

'I've tried not to let you see what a rotten time I was having.'

'I know. I'm very grateful to you. You've been awfully kind to me. Listen, Guy, I want to tell you again that I don't blame you for a single thing you did. After all, you were only a boy, and you did 830 no more than the others; I know what the loneliness is here. Oh, my dear, I'm so dreadfully sorry for you. I knew all that from the beginning. That's why I asked you for six months. My common sense tells me that I'm making a mountain out of a molehill. I'm unreasonable; I'm being unfair to you. But, you see, common 835 sense has nothing to do with it; my whole soul is in revolt. When I see the woman and her children in the village I just feel my legs shaking. Everything in this house; when I think of that bed I slept in it gives me goose-flesh. . . . You don't know what I've endured.' 840

'I think I've persuaded her to go away. And I've applied for a transfer.'

'That wouldn't help. She'll be there always. You belong to them, you don't belong to me. I think perhaps I could have stood it if there'd only been one child, but three; and the boys are quite 845 big boys. For ten years you lived with her.' And now she came out

XI with what she had been working up to. She was desperate. 'It's a physical thing, I can't help it, it's stronger than I am. I think of those thin black arms of hers round you and it fills me with a physical nausea. I think of you holding those little black babies in 850 your arms. Oh, it's loathsome. The touch of you is odious to me. Each night, when I've kissed you, I've had to brace myself up to it, I've had to clench my hands and force myself to touch your cheek.' Now she was clasping and unclasping her fingers in a nervous agony, and her voice was out of control. 'I know it's I 855 who am to blame now. I'm a silly, hysterical woman. I thought I'd get over it. I can't, and now I never shall. I've brought it all on myself; I'm willing to take the consequences; if you say I must stay here, I'll stay, but if I stay I shall die. I beseech you to let me go.'   860

And now the tears which she had restrained so long over-flowed and she wept broken-heartedly. He had never seen her cry before.

'Of course I don't want to keep you here against your will,' he said hoarsely.   865

Exhausted, she leaned back in her chair. Her features were all twisted and awry. It was horribly painful to see the abandonment of grief on that face which was habitually so placid.

'I'm so sorry, Guy. I've broken your life, but I've broken mine too. And we might have been so happy.'   870

'When do you want to go? On Tuesday?'

'Yes.'

She looked at him piteously. He buried his face in his hands. At last he looked up.

'I'm tired out,' he muttered.   875

'May I go?'

'Yes.'

For two minutes perhaps they sat there without a word. She started when the chik-chak gave its piercing, hoarse, and strangely human cry. Guy rose and went out on to the veranda.   880
He leaned against the rail and looked at the softly flowing water. He heard Doris go into her room.

Next morning, up earlier than usual, he went to her door and knocked.

'Yes?'   885

'I have to go up-river today. I shan't be back till late.'

'All right.'

She understood. He had arranged to be away all day in order not to be about while she was packing. It was heartbreaking work. When she had packed her clothes she looked round the   890
sitting-room at the things that belonged to her. It seemed dreadful to take them. She left everything but the photograph of her mother. Guy did not come in till ten o'clock at night.

'I'm sorry I couldn't get back to dinner,' he said. 'The headman at the village I had to go to had a lot of things for me to attend to.'   895

She saw his eyes wander about the room and notice that her mother's photograph no longer stood in its place.

'Is everything quite ready?' he asked. 'I've ordered the boatman to be at the steps at dawn.'

'I told the boy to wake me at five.'   900

'I'd better give you some money.' He went to his desk and wrote a cheque. He took some notes from a drawer. 'Here's some cash to take you as far as Singapore and at Singapore you'll be able to change the cheque.'

'Thank you.'   905

'Would you like me to come to the mouth of the river with you?'

'Oh, I think it would be better if we said good-bye here.'

'All right. I think I shall turn in. I've had a long day and I'm dead beat.'

He did not even touch her hand. He went into his room. In a 910 few minutes she heard him throw himself on his bed. For a little while she sat looking for the last time round that room in which she had been so happy and so miserable. She sighed deeply. She got up and went into her own room. Everything was packed except the one or two things she needed for the night.   915

It was dark when the boy awakened them. They dressed hurriedly and when they were ready breakfast was waiting for them. Presently they heard the boat row up to the landing-stage below the bungalow, and then the servants carried down her luggage. It was a poor pretence they made of eating. The 920 darkness thinned away and the river was ghostly. It was not yet day, but it was no longer night. In the silence the voices of the natives at the landing-stage were very clear. Guy glanced at his wife's untouched plate.

'If you've finished we might stroll down. I think you ought to 925 be starting.'

She did not answer. She rose from the table. She went into her room to see that nothing had been forgotten and then side by side with him walked down the steps. A little winding path led them to the river. At the landing-stage the native guards in their smart 930 uniform were lined up and they presented arms as Guy and Doris passed. The head boatman gave her his hand as she stepped into

XII the boat. She turned and looked at Guy. She wanted desperately to say one last word of comfort, once more to ask for his forgiveness, but she seemed to be struck dumb.   935

He stretched out his hand.

'Well, good-bye, I hope you'll have a jolly journey.'

They shook hands.

Guy nodded to the head boatman and the boat pushed off. The dawn now was creeping along the river mistily, but the night 940 lurked still in the dark trees of the jungle. He stood at the landing-stage till the boat was lost in the shadows of the morning. With a sigh he turned away. He nodded absent-mindedly when the guard once more presented arms. But when he reached the bungalow he called the boy. He went round the room picking out 945 everything that had belonged to Doris.

'Pack all these things up,' he said. 'It's no good leaving them about.'

Then he sat down on the veranda and watched the day advance gradually like a bitter, an unmerited, and an overwhelming 950 sorrow. At last he looked at his watch. It was time for him to go to the office.

In the afternoon he could not sleep, his head ached miserably, so he took his gun and went for a tramp in the jungle. He shot nothing, but he walked in order to tire himself out. Towards 955 sunset he came back and had two or three drinks, and then it was time to dress for dinner. There wasn't much use in dressing now; he might just as well be comfortable; he put on a loose native jacket and a sarong. That was what he had been accustomed to wear before Doris came. He was barefoot. He ate his dinner 960 listlessly and the boy cleared away and went. He sat down to read the *Tatler*. The bungalow was very silent. He could not read and let the paper fall on his knees. He was exhausted. He could not think and his mind was strangely vacant. The chik-chak was noisy that night and its hoarse and sudden cry seemed to mock 965 him. You could hardly believe that this reverberating sound came from so small a throat. Presently he heard a discreet cough.

'Who's there?' he cried.

There was a pause. He looked at the door. The chik-chak
XIII   laughed harshly. A small boy sidled in and stood on the 970 threshold. It was a little half-caste boy in a tattered singlet and a sarong. It was the elder of his two sons.

'What do you want?' said Guy.

The boy came forward into the room and sat down, tucking his legs away under him. 975

'My mother sent me. She says, do you want anything?'

Guy looked at the boy intently. The boy said nothing more. He sat and waited, his eyes cast down shyly. Then Guy in deep and bitter reflection buried his face in his hands. What was the use? It was finished. Finished! He surrendered. He sat back in his chair 980 and sighed deeply.

'Tell your mother to pack up her things and yours. She can come back.'

'When?' asked the boy, impassively.

Hot tears trickled down Guy's funny, round spotty face. 985

'Tonight.'

2 Divide into groups of six. Then divide into sub-groups of three and appoint a spokesperson in each sub-group. Decide on sides to discuss the topics:

A   Guy is wrong. He should have told Doris about his past before he married her.

B   Doris is wrong. She should have forgiven Guy for his honesty and sincerity and responded to his love and kindness.

Prepare for 15 minutes, and then present your arguments. Speakers from the opposition may interrupt if the spokesperson allows it.

3 As a class discuss informally, with your teacher as chairperson, the rights and wrongs of the two characters, Guy and Doris. This time you are invited to give your own opinion, not to argue a case. Your teacher will select the first speaker.

4 'The Force of Circumstance' may also be studied for another purpose, namely the selection of *pivotal points*. These are incidents, or actions, or conversations, or comments by the author, which mark a significant development in the story as a whole. Every story has such points, and it is likely that fluent readers would largely (but not necessarily totally) agree on what the points are. Certain areas of the text above have been shaded and numbered *I–XIII*.

The 'pivotal point' must first be identified, though in reading (as opposed to study) it is possible that we do not recognise its full significance until we have read much further. It is this which causes all readers, including native speakers, sometimes to look back and check on an earlier 'pivot'. This almost invariably indicates a heightened awareness of its significance, but an imperfect memory of the exact wording of the 'pivot'.

Now look at the first shaded area, the first 'pivotal point', marked *I*. The precise limits of the 'pivot' are not, of course, marked in any way: a few lines may be added or taken away.

We now move on to *labelling*, that is summarising the point (not the story) in just 3 or 4 words. *I* may be labelled:

Argument with Malay woman.

If we now ask 'What is the significance of the point?' the answer would probably be:

Evidence of some problem(s) in Guy's life.

There are two things to note here:

a) the significance may not be clear until we have read further into the story, or finished the story;

b) there is no single correct answer.

Take the remaining 'pivotal points' (*II–XIII*) and with your teacher's help label them, and then give a brief explanation of the significance of each one.

If you then combine all the labels, and the statements about their significance, you will have a summary of the story (cf. Unit 1). Combining them may require extensive changes of syntax. Does the summary help you to explain why you like or dislike this story?

EXPLOITATION

1 How would you explain the title 'The Force of Circumstance'?

2 'Pivotal points' sometimes coincide with an emotional heightening in the narrative. Feelings and reactions will be marked in vocabulary which will be 'strong' (i.e. have marked positive or negative associations). See particularly Unit 6. Study a number of 'pivotal points' in 'The Force of Circumstance' by seeking out words and marking them along a scale of ★–★★★★★. (For example, in *I* we

might mark the attitude of Guy in the following way: 'waylay' ★★★ (compare: stop); 'vexed' ★★★ (compare: cross or perturbed); 'surreptitious' ★★★ (compare: unnoticed). You will need to make use of a dictionary and to consult with your teacher.

3 Find other stories by Somerset Maugham. Isolate 'pivotal points'. Use reference to these 'pivots' to help you decide which story you prefer and why.

4 'An object is lost, and then recovered.'
'A settlement is disrupted, and ultimately restored.'
Continuing the psychological analysis of Unit 9, which of these statements more nearly 'fits' the story 'The Force of Circumstance'? Explain the story in terms of what is lost, or what is disrupted.

5 Re-read the story 'Cat in the Rain', Unit 1, *Summary I*. Divide into groups of six. Then divide into sub-groups of three and appoint a spokesperson in each sub-group. Decide on sides and discuss the following statements about 'the American wife' and her husband George in 'Cat in the Rain':

A George is level-headed and contented. His wife cannot settle and is neurotic. She behaves like a little child and George has to be firm with her. The rift in the relationship is the wife's fault.

B George is selfish and insensitive to his wife's needs. She wants more care and attention. The rift in the relationship is George's fault.

Forum IV

1 Divide into groups of six. Then, as background, 'pool' (i.e. put together) your collective knowledge of the Victorian period.
When did it begin and end?
Who were the main literary figures of the period in England?
What were their concerns?
What was the religious background to their writing?
What were the socio-economic conditions in England?
In what way(s) did these affect literary production?
   For the above you should use library facilities and resource persons, as available.

2 Listen to these three poems before you read them.

Rest

O EARTH, lie heavily upon her eyes;
Seal her sweet eyes weary of watching, Earth;
   Lie close around her; leave no room for mirth
With its harsh laughter, nor for sound of sighs.
She hath no questions, she hath no replies,   5
   Hush'd in and curtain'd with a blessed dearth
   Of all that irk'd her from the hour of birth;
With stillness that is almost Paradise.
Darkness more clear than noonday holdeth her,
   Silence more musical than any song;   10
Even her very heart has ceased to stir:
Until the morning of Eternity
Her rest shall not begin nor end, but be;
   And when she wakes she will not think it long.

Christina Georgina Rossetti

The Dead Child

BUT yesterday she played with childish things,
   With toys and painted fruit.
To-day she may be speeding on bright wings
   Beyond the stars! We ask. The stars are mute.

But yesterday her doll was all in all;   5
   She laughed and was content.
To-day she will not answer, if we call:
   She dropp'd no toys to show the road she went.

But yesterday she smiled and ranged with art
   Her playthings on the bed.   10
To-day and yesterday are leagues apart!
   She will not smile to-day, for she is dead.

George Barlow

Margaritae Sorori, I.M.

A LATE lark twitters from the quiet skies;
And from the west,
Where the sun, his day's work ended,
Lingers as in content
There falls on the old, gray city   5
An influence luminous and serene,
A shining peace.

The smoke ascends
In a rosy-and-golden haze. The spires
Shine, and are changed. In the valley   10
Shadows rise. The lark sings on. The sun,
Closing his benediction,
Sinks, and the darkening air
Thrills with a sense of the triumphing night—
Night with her train of stars   15
And her great gift of sleep.

So be my passing!
My task accomplish'd and the long day done,
My wages taken, and in my heart
Some late lark singing,   20
Let me be gather'd to the quiet west,
The sundown splendid and serene,
Dead.

William Ernest Henley

3 Students of literature are usually asked to read and study 'established favourites'
but the three poems above are relatively little known. This section is intended to
open up more informal discussion and debate about less well-known works.
  The topics for discussion are as follows:

A Death is an almost taboo (forbidden) subject in daily conversation, but is an
   appropriate subject for poetry. These three poems give an interesting
   comment on the subject.

B The Victorians were obsessed with the thought of death, and this rubbish
   (i.e. these three poems) is a typical example.

Within your groups divide into sub-groups of three, and appoint a spokesperson
in each sub-group. Decide on sides. Prepare for 15 minutes, and then present
your arguments. Speakers from the opposition may interrupt if the spokesperson
allows it.

EXPLOITATION

Listen to the cassette again. Prepare for 15 minutes, then choose the first speaker.
As a class, and with your teacher as chairperson, discuss the relative merits of the
three poems in *Forum IV*. You are invited to make a completely subjective
judgement as to which poem is the best and which second best. You should be able
to support your judgement by reference to the text. Units 1, 2 and 3 in particular,
should help you to find ways to justify your choice.

Forum V

Here again, as in *Forum I* and *II* we are going to put a particular section of life or society under the microscope. This time, however, there is one important difference. The discussions arising out of the Shakespeare texts deal with 'universal' themes. The subjects are almost equally applicable at all times and in totally different societies. This is common in Shakespearean drama, which is one of the reasons why it is still so widely read, studied and performed. The following poem is on a more local and topical subject. It describes a section of society in Britain in the 1950s, when the poem was written. It is therefore suitable for comparing and contrasting with other societies at other times. The poem is by Vernon Scannell (born 1922) and is called 'Schoolroom on a Wet Afternoon'. The subject is contemporary youth and education and opens the way to general discussion on these topics.

1 Listen to this poem before you read it.

        Schoolroom on a Wet Afternoon

        The unrelated paragraphs of morning
        Are forgotten now: the severed heads of kings
        Rot by the misty Thames: the roses of York
        And Lancaster are pressed between the leaves
        Of history; negroes sleep in Africa.   5
        The complexities of simple interest lurk
        In inkwells and the brittle sticks of chalk:
        Afternoon is come and English Grammar.

Rain falls as though the sky has been bereaved,
Stutters its inarticulate grief on glass   10
Of every lachrymose pane. The children read
Their books or make pretence of concentration,
Each bowed head seems bent in supplication
Or resignation to the fate that waits
In the unmapped forests of the future.   15
Is it their doomed innocence noon weeps for?

In each diminutive breast a human heart
Pumps out the necessary blood: desires,
Pains and ecstasies surfride each singing wave
Which breaks in darkness on the mental shores.   20
Each child is disciplined; absorbed and still
At his small desk. Yet lift the lid and see,
Amidst frayed books and pencils, other shapes:
Vicious rope, glaring blade, the gun cocked to kill.

Vernon Scannell

2 We suggest the class should sit in a half circle, with the teacher acting as
chairperson. Any member of the class may begin the discussion. You are invited
to express your opinion, using the poem as a starting point. Each presentation
should be about two minutes. Other members of the group may interrupt if the
speaker allows it. You are not discussing a single topic, but a variety of topics
suggested by the poem. For example:
a) Only in the depressed areas of large cities are children like this.
b) If modern youngsters are vicious it is modern society which has made them
   so.
c) Children are not interested in lessons because the great majority of textbooks
   are extremely dull.
Extend this list to at least six topics (and preferably ten) before you begin. Then
speak about any of them, but try not to repeat what any previous speaker has said.

EXPLOITATION

Re-read the poem 'The Village Schoolmaster' (Unit 3, *Ranking I*). There is a point
of similarity in the words:
    'A man severe he was' (Goldsmith) and
    'Each child is disciplined' (Vernon Scannell)
but thereafter most of the differences are suggested (implicit rather than explicit) in
these two very different poems. Write a paragraph saying what these differences
are. If you had not been told who had written either poem, or when, how would
you know that one poem described a modern situation?

SUMMARY OF THE UNIT

1 This final unit has attempted to encourage you to combine the approaches you have practised in the previous units.
2 The focus in the case of 'The Force of Circumstance' is on a longer text. Your work on it should encourage you and give you confidence to continue to read longer texts: complete plays, long poems and novels.
3 You have discussed the themes raised by the text and related them to contemporary social, political and moral issues. You have debated other people's viewpoints and perhaps come to understand your own better. This is one of the values of reading literature and we hope you will have opportunities for further discussion as you read more.
4 You have also been encouraged to say what you like and dislike about the texts. It would be a good idea for you now to re-read some of the texts in this book you particularly liked or disliked and try to give an account of your reactions.

Our aim has been to encourage you to respond and react to literature. We hope you will continue to do this and continue to support your views with precise analysis of the language. Remember there is much more to literature than just language and you should try to integrate your studies of language and literature.

GOOD READING!

Appendices

1 They were leisurely enough for him to take in the full meaning of the portent, and to taste the flavour of death rising in his gorge. His wife had gone raving mad—murdering mad. They were leisurely enough for the first paralysing effect of this discovery to pass away before a resolute determination to come out victorious   5 from the ghastly struggle with that armed lunatic. They were leisurely enough for Mr. Verloc to elaborate a plan of defence involving a dash behind the table, and the felling of the woman to the ground with a heavy wooden chair. But they were not leisurely enough to allow Mr. Verloc the time to move either hand   10 or foot. The knife was already planted in his breast. It met no resistance on its way. Hazard has such accuracies. Into that plunging blow, delivered over the side of the couch, Mrs. Verloc had put all the inheritance of her immemorial and obscure descent, the simple ferocity of the age of caverns, and the   15 unbalanced nervous fury of the age of bar-rooms. Mr. Verloc, the Secret Agent, turning slightly on his side with the force of the blow, expired without stirring a limb, in the muttered sound of the word "Don't" by way of protest.

Joseph Conrad: *The Secret Agent*

2 His fine instincts made him turn his head away and assume an attitude of negligent contemplation, with his ears and mind alive to every sound behind him.

"Goodness!" said a voice, with a sharp note of surprise.

Mr. Polly was on his feet in an instant. "Dear me! Can I be of   5 any assistance?" he said, with deferential gallantry.

"I don't know," said the young lady, and regarded him calmly with clear blue eyes. "I didn't know there was any one there," she added.

"Sorry," said Mr. Polly, "if I am intrudacious. I didn't know you   10 didn't want me to be here."

She reflected for a moment on the word.

"It isn't that," she said, surveying him. "I oughtn't to get over the wall," she explained. "It's out of bounds; at least in term time. But this being holidays—" 15

Her manner placed the matter before him.

"Holidays is different," said Mr. Polly.

"I don't want to actually *break* the rules," she said.

"Leave them behind you," said Mr. Polly, with a catch of the breath, "where they are safe." And marvelling at his own wit and 20 daring, and indeed trembling within himself, he held out a hand for her.

She brought another brown leg from the unknown, and arranged her skirt with a dexterity altogether feminine.

"I think I'll stay on the wall," she decided. "So long as some of 25 me's in bounds—"

She continued to regard him with an irresistible smile of satisfaction. Mr. Polly smiled in return.

"You bicycle?" she said.

Mr. Polly admitted the fact, and she said she did too. 30

"All my people are in India," she explained. "It's beastly rot—I mean it's frightfully dull being left here alone."

"All *my* people," said Mr. Polly, "are in Heaven!"

"I say!"

"Fact," said Mr. Polly. "Got nobody." 35

"And that's why—" She checked her artless comment on his mourning. "I say," she said in a sympathetic voice, "I *am* sorry. I really am. Was it a fire, or a ship—or something?"

Her sympathy was very delightful. He shook his head. "The ordinary tables of mortality," he said. "First one, and then 40 another."

Behind this outward melancholy, delight was dancing wildly:

"Are *you* lonely?" asked the girl.

Mr. Polly nodded.

"I was just sitting there in melancholic rectrospectatiousness," 45 he said, indicating the logs; and again a swift thoughtfulness swept across her face.

"There's no harm in our talking," she reflected.

"It's a kindness. Won't you get down?"

She reflected, and surveyed the turf below and the scene 50 around, and him.

"I'll stay on the wall," she said, "if only for bounds' sake."

She certainly looked quite adorable on the wall. She had a fine neck and pointed chin that was particularly admirable from below, and pretty eyes and fine eyebrows are never so pretty as 55 when they look down upon one. But no calculation of that sort, thank Heaven, was going on beneath her ruddy shock of hair.

H. G. Wells: *The History of Mr. Polly*

3 What then can move her? if nor merth nor mone,
  she is no woman, but a sencelesse stone.

Edmund Spenser

4 Yes, lad, I lie easy,
  I lie as lads would choose;
I cheer a dead man's sweetheart,
  Never ask me whose.

A. E. Housman

5 ONCE upon a time there will be a little girl called Uncumber.
 Uncumber will have a younger brother called Sulpice, and they
will live with their parents in a house in the middle of the woods.
There will be no windows in the house, because there will be
nothing to see outside except the forest. While inside there will be 5
all kinds of interesting things – strange animals, processions,
jewels, battles, mazes, convolutions of pure shapes and pure
colours – which materialise in the air at will, solid and brilliant
and almost touchable. For this will be in the good new days a
long, long while ahead, and it will be like that in people's houses 10
then. So the sight of the mud and grimy leaves outside would
scarcely be of much interest.
 Then again, windows might let the air in, and no one would
want the congenial atmosphere of the house contaminated by the
stale, untempered air of the forest, laden with dust and disease. 15
From one year's end to the next they won't go outside, and the
outside world won't come in. There will be no need; all their food
and medicine and jewellery and toys will be on tap from the
mains – everything they could possibly require will come to the
house through the network of pipes and tubes and wires and 20
electromagnetic beams which tangle the forest. Out along the
wires and beams their wishes will go back. Back, by return, will
come the fulfilment of them.

Michael Frayn: *A Very Private Life*

6   The car ploughed uphill through the long squalid straggle of
Tevershall, the blackened brick dwellings, the black slate roofs
glistening their sharp edges, the mud black with coal-dust, the
pavements wet and black. It was as if dismalness had soaked
through and through everything. The utter negation of natural 5
beauty, the utter negation of the gladness of life, the utter

absence of the instinct for shapely beauty which every bird and
beast has, the utter death of the human intuitive faculty was
appalling. The stacks of soap in the grocers' shops, the rhubarb
and lemons in the greengrocers! the awful hats in the milliners! 10
all went by ugly, ugly, ugly, followed by the plaster-and-gilt
horror of the cinema with its wet picture announcements, 'A
Woman's Love!', and the new big Primitive chapel, primitive
enough in its stark brick and big panes of greenish and
raspberry glass in the windows. The Wesleyan chapel, higher 15
up, was of blackened brick and stood behind iron railings and
blackened shrubs. The Congregational chapel, which thought
itself superior, was built of rusticated sandstone and had a
steeple, but not a very high one. Just beyond were the new
school buildings, expensive pink brick, and gravelled play- 20
ground inside iron railings, all very imposing, and mixing the
suggestion of a chapel and a prison. Standard Five girls were
having a singing lesson, just finishing the la-me-doh-la
exercises and beginning a 'sweet children's song'. Anything
more unlike song, spontaneous song, would be impossible to 25
imagine: a strange bawling yell that followed the outlines of a
tune. It was not like savages: savages have subtle rhythms. It
was not like animals: animals *mean* something when they yell.
It was like nothing on earth, and it was called singing.

D. H. Lawrence: *Lady Chatterley's Lover*

7

Futility

Move him into the sun—
Gently its touch awoke him once,
At home, whispering of fields unsown.
Always it woke him, even in France,
Until this morning and this snow.   5
If anything might rouse him now
The kind old sun will know.

Think how it wakes the seeds,—
Woke, once, the clays of a cold star.
Are limbs, so dear-achieved, are sides,   10
Full-nerved—still warm—too hard to stir?
Was it for this the clay grew tall?
—O what made fatuous sunbeams toil
To break earth's sleep at all?

Wilfred Owen

8

There's been a Death, in the Opposite House,
    As lately as Today —
I know it, by the numb look
    Such Houses have — alway —

The Neighbors rustle in and out —   5
    The Doctor — drives away —
A Window opens like a Pod —
    Abrupt — mechanically —

Somebody flings a Mattress out —
    The Children hurry by —   10
They wonder if it died — on that —
    I used to — when a Boy —

The Minister — goes stiffly in —
    As if the House were His —
And He owned all the Mourners — now —   15
    And little Boys — besides —

And then the Milliner — and the Man
    Of the Appalling Trade —
To take the measure of the House —
    There'll be that Dark Parade —   20

Of Tassels — and of Coaches — soon —
    It's easy as a Sign —
The Intuition of the News —
    In just a Country Town —

Emily Dickinson

9

A narrow Fellow in the Grass
Occasionally rides —
You may have met Him — did you not
His notice sudden is —

The Grass divides as with a Comb —   5
A spotted shaft is seen —
And then it closes at your feet
And opens further on —

He likes a Boggy Acre
A Floor too cool for Corn —   10
Yet when a Boy, and Barefoot —
I more than once at Noon

Have passed, I thought, a Whip lash
Unbraiding in the Sun
When stooping to secure it   15
It wrinkled, and was gone –

Several of Nature's People
I know, and they know me –
I feel for them a transport
Of cordiality –   20

But never met this Fellow
Attended, or alone
Without a tighter breathing
And Zero at the Bone –

Emily Dickinson

Acknowledgements

The authors and publishers are grateful to the authors, publishers and others who have given permission for the use of copyright material identified in the text. It has not been possible to identify the sources of all the material used and in such cases the publishers would welcome information from copyright owners.

The Observer, London for the extract from 'Expert aims to salvage détente from ocean bed' by Alan Road (12.10.86) on pp. 5–6; The Executors of the Ernest Hemingway Estate, and Jonathan Cape Ltd for 'Cat in the Rain' from *The First Forty-Nine Stories* by Ernest Hemingway on pp. 6–8; *Cambridge Evening News* for the extract from 'Driver crushed to death on line' by Mila Vucevic (3.7.86) on p. 13; The Estate of Joseph Conrad for the extracts from *The Secret Agent* on pp. 14 and 181, and 'Youth' on pp. 61–2; A. P. Watt Ltd on behalf of The Literary Executors of the Estate of H. G. Wells for the extract from *The History of Mr Polly* by H. G. Wells on pp. 14–16 and 181–2; The Society of Authors as literary representative of the Estate of A. E. Housman, and Jonathan Cape Ltd, publishers of A. E. Housman's *Collected Poems* for 'Is my team ploughing' on pp. 18–19 and 183; Methuen London for *Last to Go* from *A Slight Ache and Other Plays* by Harold Pinter on pp. 28–31, and 'Reported Missing' from *Moonsearch* by Bary Cole on p. 106; Longman Singapore Publications Ltd for the extract from *Readthru* by Long and Nation on p. 43; A. P. Watt Ltd on behalf of Michael B. Yeats and Macmillan London Ltd for 'An Irish Airman Foresees His Death' by W. B. Yeats on p. 46; Laurence Pollinger Ltd and the Estate of Mrs Frieda Lawrence Ravagli for 'Snake' on pp. 50–3, and the extracts from *Lady Chatterley's Lover* on pp. 89–90, 103, 183–4; George Sassoon for 'The General' by Siegfried Sassoon on p. 55; A. P. Watt Ltd on behalf of Lady Herbert for 'After the Battle' by A. P. Herbert on pp. 59–60 and 135; Muriel Spark for the extract from *The Prime of Miss Jean Brodie* on p. 63; Carcanet Press Ltd for 'Spacepoem 3: Off Course' from *Poems of Thirty Years* by Edwin Morgan on p. 66; The Literary Estate of Virginia Woolf, and The Hogarth Press for the extract from *Mrs Dalloway* by Virginia Woolf on pp. 76–7; Collins for the extract from *A Very Private Life* by Michael Frayn on pp. 88 and 183; Austin Rover Group Ltd and Leo Burnett Ltd for the advertisement on p. 95; Victor Gollancz Ltd for the extracts from *Lucky Jim* by Kingsley Amis on p. 96, and *One Day in the Life of Ivan Denisovich* on pp. 139–40, and *The White Hotel* by D. M. Thomas on pp. 142–3; British Telecom for the user instructions on p. 97; Oxford University Press for the extracts from 'A Martian Sends a Postcard Home' from *A Martian Sends a Postcard Home* by Craig Raine, © Craig Raine 1979 on p. 98, and 'Stylistics' by Henry Widdowson in *Techniques in Applied Linguistics* vol. 3 edited by J. P. B. Allen and S. Pit Corder 1974 on p. 115; Thomson Holidays for the extract from their *Winter Sun and Cities* brochure 1982–83 on pp. 99–100; A. P. Watt Ltd on behalf of The Royal Literary Fund, and William Heinemann Ltd for 'The Force of Circumstance' by W. Somerset Maugham on pp. 102, 128, 152–73; Scandinavian Airlines for the advertisement on p. 107; The Estate of Wilfred Owen, and Chatto & Windus for 'Futility' by Wilfred Owen on pp. 110–11 and 184; Edward Arnold (Publishers) Ltd for the extract from *Modern Poetry: Studies in Practical Criticism* by C. B. Cox and A. E. Dyson on p. 115; Reprinted by permission of the publishers and the Trustees of Amherst College from *The Poems of Emily Dickinson*, edited by Thomas H. Johnson, Cambridge, Mass.: The Belknap Press of Harvard University Press, copyright 1951, © 1955, 1979, 1983 by The President and Fellows of Harvard College for 'There's been a Death, in the opposite house' on pp. 115–16 and 185, and 'A narrow Fellow in the Grass' on pp. 117 and 185–6; Macmillan London Ltd for 'The Oxen' on p. 119, and 'As I Set Out for Lyonnesse' by Thomas Hardy on p. 130; *The Daily Telegraph* for "'Dingo' Appeal Rejected" by Dennis Warner (30.4.83) on pp. 125–6; Andre Deutsch Ltd and Alfred A. Knopf, Inc. for the extract from *The Centaur* by John Updike (1963 edition) on p. 127; Reprinted by permission of Penguin Books Ltd, the extract from *Young Thomas Hardy* by Robert Gittings (Penguin Books, pp. 180–1), copyright © Robert Gittings, 1975, 1978 on pp. 129–30; Basil Blackwell Ltd for the extract from *Literary Theory* by Terry Eagleton on p. 141; Robson Books Ltd for 'Schoolroom on a Wet Afternoon' from *New and Collected Poems 1950–1980* by Vernon Scannel on pp. 178–9.

Photographs and illustrations: Doug James p. 10; Will Green from *Illustrated Teach Yourself: Cats* Hodder & Stoughton Children's Books p. 10; MAGPAS p. 13; The Mansell Collection pp. 23 and 133; Oxford University Press for the illustration from *The Oxford Illustrated Dickens*, 1966 (with illustrations from the 1885 edition) p. 33; Sheffield City Libraries for *Sheffield from the South-East* by W. M. Ibbitt p. 47; Chichester Festival Theatre production photograph by Zoe Dominic p. 58; The Illustrated London News Picture Library p. 61; NASA p. 65; John Love for the illustration from *The Return of the Sea Eagle* Cambridge University Press p. 72; David Mostyn p. 83; Barnaby's Picture Library pp. 99, 117, 151; National Museums of Scotland p. 110; Macmillan, London and Basingstoke for the map from *Hardy's Wessex* by Desmond Hawkins p. 131; Imperial War Museum p. 136; BBC Hulton Picture Library p. 178.

Index of authors and works

Numbers in bold refer to printed works, numbers in lighter type indicate additional tasks.